In-Between

Exploring small cracks of everyday life

Karen Ida Dannesboe & Jon Dag Rasmussen eds.

In-Between

Exploring small cracks of everyday life

Aarhus University Press

In-Between. Exploring small cracks of everyday life
© The Authors and Aarhus University Press 2021

Cover: Camilla Jørgensen, Trefold
Layout and typesetting: Narayana Press
Publishing editor: Sanne Lind Hansen
This book is typeset in Adobe Garamond and printed
on 115 g Munken Premium Cream 13
Printed by Narayana Press, Denmark

Printed in Denmark 2021

ISBN 978 87 7219 138 6
ISSN 2245 2737

Anthropological Studies vol. 7

Aarhus University Press
aarhusuniversitypress.dk

Published with the financial support of
Aarhus University Research Foundation

All rights reserved. Except for the quotation of short passages for the purpose of criticism and review, no part of this publication may be reproduced, stored in a retrieval system, or transmitted, in any form or by any means, without the prior permission of the publisher.

International distributors

Oxbow Books Ltd., oxbowbooks.com
ISD, isdistribution.com

PEER
REVIEWED

/ In accordance with requirements of the Danish Ministry of Higher Education and Science, the certification means that a PhD level peer has made a written assessment justifying this book's scientific quality.

Contents

Foreword   7

CHAPTER 1:
Pocket-ethnography and the study of in-between phenomena   9
Jon Dag Rasmussen & Karen Ida Dannesboe

CHAPTER 2:
'The hand in the mouth': stories from a shared body   25
Naja Dahlstrup Mogensen

CHAPTER 3:
The sense and place of sand in day care   43
Nanna Jordt Jørgensen

CHAPTER 4:
Attunement to school and classmates   59
Karen Ida Dannesboe

CHAPTER 5:
The companion city – an initial ramble   71
Jon Dag Rasmussen

CHAPTER 6:
Designing place through rhythms and affinities   89
Anne-Lene Sand

CHAPTER 7:
The house: being, seeing, remembering place 107
Ida Wentzel Winther

AFTERWORD:
The micro-physics of mornings 119
Orvar Löfgren

Author information 130

Foreword

The genesis of this anthology has been a slow process, progressing over a number of years. It is a product of empirical, theoretical and epistemological interests shared by a group of researchers. The contributing authors are all members of a small cross-university research collective that operates under the name *Mellemrum*, a Danish term signifying the space in-between (something, someone, somebody/bodies), of which an English equivalent might be the concept of *interstices*. This collective was established in 2014 on the initiative of Associate Professor Ida Wentzel Winther with the ambition of promoting informal and cross-university collaboration between a group of scholars related to the Department of Educational Anthropology at the Danish School of Education, Aarhus University. The group comprises researchers who are all engaged in ethnographic explorations of places, people and senses, and with a wide range of phenomena that emerge in everyday life situations – in-between humans, materials, non-humans and various practices and daily chores. The participating researchers are invested in fields spanning from early childhood studies and youth studies to family studies and studies of elderly members of society. One of the collective's core motivations is an ongoing interest in experimenting with academic genres and research dissemination, and in testing, bending and challenging the standards and rules of academic practice. In the spirit of the work carried out in *Mellemrum* since its inception, we want to use the space provided by the pages of this book to pause, to allow ourselves to stop, dwell on and pursue the trivial and seemingly insignificant small phenomena of everyday life.

The book, like the work carried out in *Mellemrum*, is influenced by a number of different theoretical ideas, strands of thought and interests. This multitude of influences is clearly reflected in the chapters of the book. Despite this breadth, we also share a number of references that (in)form our thinking, our work and the writing displayed in this anthology. Some of the generative process were inspired by our joint reading and discussion of the sociologist Jennifer Mason's work on affinities (2018). Mason's book contributed, among other theoretical and epistemological interests, to a shared curiosity regarding the exploration of more ephemeral, uneven, unexplainable and uncategorizable parts of our research material and our interests. Furthermore, the work of anthropologist and thinker Tim Ingold has had a major impact on the ideas generated and the work carried out in the collective endeavours of *Mellemrum*.

We want to thank the contributing authors for ongoing discussions and patience as the book has progressed over the past few years. A warm thanks to Orvar Löfgren for writing a thoughtful epilogue pointing to the relevance of studying the unnoticed cracks. Furthermore, we wish to thank Anne-Lene Sand for her contribution to the introductory chapter in the first part of the process, the series editor at Aarhus University Press, Sanne Lind Hansen, for her work and her belief in the project at an early stage, as well as the anonymous peer-reviewer of the manuscript for relevant, applicable and supportive comments. The anthology was made possible by the support of our respective research institutions and with generous funding granted by the Research Fund of Aarhus University.

We sincerely hope that the book will find a broad audience, that it can contribute to debates within anthropology and kindred social sciences, and that it will be a source of inspiration to academics, students and laypeople alike.

Jon Dag Rasmussen & Karen Ida Dannesboe
Copenhagen, March 2021

CHAPTER 1:

Pocket-ethnography and the study of in-between phenomena

Jon Dag Rasmussen & Karen Ida Dannesboe

Standing on a pavement on a busy afternoon. The city swarms with the incessant sounds of traffic, the humming of people, shouts and fragmented conversations. A bus passes by and, for the briefest of moments, eyes meet, pedestrian and passenger. A fleeting, albeit intense, sensation occurs as the encounter pierces the moving window's transparent glass membrane. Eyes and bodies exchange stories that are at once strangely important and strangely indistinct. In a small in-between moment, the fuss and noisy atmosphere of the city seems to withdraw and disappear, leaving the pavement bathed in a mute ambience. A tiny second shared, an unexpected encounter. A strange affect sprayed into the air. A change occurring. Almost instantly the roar of the city returns at full strength; the deafening noise of construction workers and their tools, groups of shouting children, movement.

In his foreword to the book *Species of Spaces and Other Pieces*, the French author and experimentalist, Georges Perec, declares that the subject of the work in the reader's hand "… is not the void exactly, but rather what there is round about or inside it" (2008, p. 5). The world we inhabit is not just a single entirety, Perec continues. Instead, it swarms with myriad small compartments, experiential cracks and bits – "and one of these bits is a Métro corridor, and another of them is a public park" (ibid., p. 6). Yet another such bit is the situational crack that materializes and unexpectedly connects two strangers, as described in the opening fragment above. This fragment highlights how sudden bends in everyday atmospheres occur out of 'nowhere', and how coincidental micro-meetings between people can carry a both indistinct and enormous weight. Such casual encounters can be charged and saturated with surprising, imprecise and indefinable meaning, while leaving a mark, or an impression, that lasts much longer. The everyday lives we lead as human beings are filled with numerous voids and gaps, situations and small cracks – occurrences and experiences that emerge, last for short or longer periods of time and perish once again. Some of these are perceived only fleetingly – they tend to be almost imperceptible or to unfold in registers that remain at the borders of what we are able to pin down and account for in words. Meanwhile, such fleeting experiences remain a central constituent of our lifeworlds. This also makes such phenomena and experiential cracks a highly relevant and important field to study ethnographically.

The aim of this book is to contribute to the study of small, withdrawn and otherwise unnoticed parts of everyday life as they are encountered through ethnographic fieldwork. The chapters explore phenomena of a minor and seemingly trivial character or stature: cracks, crevices and particularities inherent to ordinary everyday life. A common point of departure among the contributing authors has been to question, analyse and become aware of some of the many in-between occurrences that characterize the lives and contexts we engage in as social researchers. In this sense our ambition is to approach, and to dwell among, various kinds of *micro-elements*: situations, practices and trifles that, despite initially appearing dull and of little relevance to social scientific research, majorly affect people, communities and societies at large. In this regard, we work along some of the core phenomenological currents of ethnographic fieldwork by acknowledging the myriad minor, seemingly dubious and oddly charged experiences that occur when working, and living, along the people we study. Ethnography is a remarkable and rewarding way of working whereby we often gain knowledge that exceeds our preliminary expectations in terms of both research goals and general recognition. The contributions cover a range of empirical fields, such as cities, skate parks, schools, kindergartens, homes and bodies, employing situations where people connect with one another and with their material environments, their objects and places, as a common point of departure. Compiling and working with this anthology as a research collective, we encouraged each other to dig into both new and existing empirical material exploring curious and otherwise somewhat unaccounted for phenomena. The shared interest has been to apply some of the small and indeterminate, yet evocative, fragments and remnants from previous or ongoing research projects that render themselves important despite their intangible and blurry character. We hereby aim to acknowledge experiences and findings that often reside at the periphery of our empirical knowledge, material and research projects. Small changes and charges in ordinary life situations, atmospheric slides and sudden alterations in bodily attitudes, encounters with inexplicable impulses and the experience of kinship, immediate rapport, sparks, spontaneous insights or long-term relations to non-human entities are indeed uneven and odd phenomena to encounter during fieldwork. For this reason, they tend to slip through our fingers if we fail to allocate them the necessary amount of social scientific attention. They rarely make the journey from our field journals to a life in print. Nevertheless, a substantial part of human life is touched and affected by such unnoticed, effervescent, withdrawn and yet vibrant workings of small everyday 'mysteries'. In the chapters in this anthology, we hold on to these aspects of human existence by paying close attention to moments where sand, hands, pencils, wind, human bodies, places, pasts, presents and futures connect in different ways.

Our overall ambition with the volume is to explore what happens in the unnoticed corners and domains of everyday life and to dwell on very mundane experiences and phenomena that often escape direct attention in the analytical processes of writing ethnography. Thus, the contributors to this anthology are all committed to foregrounding empirical experiences of minor stature, and to exposing unnoticed and low-pitched empirical events and phenomena to processes of textual amplification and analytical qualification. This reflects the joint ambition of presenting and disseminating knowledge, small-scale phenomena and findings distilled from the harlequin experiences acquired through ethnographic fieldwork. To this end, we are preoccupied with the idea of converting material, experiences, empirically qualified sensations and other situations that are usually considered peripheral and insignificant 'backgrounds' to analytical 'foregrounds'.

Approaching the unnoticed

Within anthropology and other cultural sciences, there is a long tradition of exploring people's everyday lives across time and space in order to understand cultural and social variations and phenomena. Studying people as social beings – the taken-for-granted parts of their engagement with each other and the worldly environment – is part of the scientific gaze and a core analytical endeavour. The interest in small elements of everyday life can be traced back to the 1930s, paying homage to a number of thinkers and researchers from this period and onwards (see e.g. Benjamin 2003, 2006; de Certeau 1984; Lefebvre 1991). These perspectives have had a major impact within the cultural sciences, especially in strands of social research focused on human-materiality relations, in disciplines such as anthropology, ethnology and qualitatively oriented sociology.

As a sub-genre of ethnographic research, the study of everyday trivialities and unnoticed parts of human practice and societies has steadily evolved over the last 25 years (e.g. Bech-Jørgensen 1994, Jacobsen 2009). Central developers of this tradition, Swedish ethnologists Billy Ehn and Orvar Löfgren explore the phenomenon of *nothingness* in their work from 2010 entitled *The secret world of doing nothing*. Besides their elegant analytical work on phenomena such as *waiting time* and other kinds of *nothingness* that reside behind the immediate facades of late-modern Western societies, they encourage students, scholars and researchers to dwell on the smaller, slower and withdrawn parts of their worlds (Ehn and Löfgren 2010, p. 217-27). Following a similar line of thought, the cultural theorist Ben Highmore (2011) argues for the necessity of studying the ordinary: the seemingly well-known habits and routines of everyday life, as well as the moods, rhythms and feelings that are part of and unfold during everyday occurrences. As he writes, this is a way to approach situations where 'nothing much' is happening, and to grasp the character of the minutiae of everyday life.

A related ambition is found in the works of anthropologist Kathleen Stewart (e.g. 2007). Stewart is committed to exposing the ephemeral and fluid elements that fill voids between the so-called 'memorable' and 'significant' events inherent to everyday human life. Her approach, both in terms of subject matter and writing style, represents a critique of the established social scientific hierarchy and its prioritization of certain phenomena and expressions of humanity over others. In Stewart's work, what she calls *ordinary affects* are small and condensed happenings that impact everyday life to a great extent as "their significance lies in the intensities they build and in what thoughts and feelings they make possible" (Stewart 2007, p. 3). Approaching kindred lines of thought from another angle, the activist philosopher Erin Manning argues that any kind of minor event, or "Minor Gesture", the title of her book from 2016, contains major political potencies and potential powers. Minor gestures are events that may pass almost unnoticed, seemingly marginal twists and turns that nevertheless possess vital powers as they enter and transform the field of relations of which they are part, carrying a potential for extensive and large-scale change and re-ordering.

With yet another approach towards the importance of seemingly small happenings, anthropologist Tim Ingold describes the world we inhabit as an intricate *meshwork* consisting of human as well as other-than-human (life)lines (2011, 2015). In his newer work Ingold is preoccupied with different kinds of relational 'clinging' (e.g. 2015) – practices in which we humans correspond, interweave with and live alongside each other and a broad field of non-human existences and things in a world that is fundamentally adrift. In clinging to things, creatures and others, we can hope to withstand the fundamental processes of continuous movement that characterize our worldly environment. These acts of clinging are often embedded in minor and trivial everyday practices, in the most common habits and doings, in everyday correspondences (cf. Ingold 2021). With a similar attention towards low-pitched and almost ineffable *affinities*, the sociologist Jennifer Mason (2018) attempts to capture and explore slippery components of social, material and non-material relationships through a *sensory-kinaesthetic attunement*. Mason's work illustrates how sensations emerge in and from social as well as socio-material contact(s) and catalyse certain affinities. Affinities are expressed and experienced in what Mason describes as "sparks" – in flows, whims and charges that materialize through connections of both transient and recurrent kinds. The notion serves as an acknowledgement of the potency of such connections, which are an integral, although often ephemeral, fuzzy and nondescript, component of human and other-than-human encounters and entanglements. Mason encourages scholars to scrutinize sensations of affinity as an object in itself. In her book *Affinities – Potent Connections in Personal Life* (2018), she creates a narrative that seems experimental and probing compared to mainstream social scientific work. She draws inspiration from the so-called sensory, affective and material turns, but also pushes against their limitations as she invites sociologists and others to adopt an *affinities orientation,* which implies openness, attentiveness and the application of a greater degree of poeticism in their work.

Working within different traditions and branches of academia, all of the scholars mentioned above promote and underline the significance of apparently small and unnoticed phenomena of everyday life. Furthermore, they all agree on the importance of various knowledge embedded in small- and micro-scale experiences and on the need to carry out studies and explorations of such occurrences emerging in the flow and routines of everyday life. This applies whether the aim is to grasp and analyse the small(est) expressions of human being, or to address larger, more general issues inherent to human and other-than-human existence and societies. A similar endeavour has emerged in a growing body of social scientific studies on materiality and affect that has evolved over the past 5-10 years. Common to these approaches is a novel attention towards senses, bodies, memories, atmospheres, things and environments when studying social and cultural worlds (e.g. Carlson & Stewart 2014; Frykman & Frykman 2016; Harvey & Knox 2014; Ingold 2011; Schroer & Schmitt 2018). Drawing on a range of such perspectives allows us to nuance, as well as to contribute to, everyday life studies that are often difficult to address using classical social scientific vocabularies (cf. Ehn & Löfgren, 2017) and therefore call for analytical and textual experiments, as well as creative writing practices (cf. Harvey and Knox 2014; Carlson & Stewart 2014). What we wish to develop is research capable of amplifying the subtle relations between humans and societal institutions, places and things by pointing to aspects of human and other-than-human worlds that fall between dominant categories and distinctions. It is research of a kind that provides knowledge of familiar places, such as a kindergarten or an urban space, with particular attention to the subtle, specific and even odd processes and connections that constantly emerge between humans and environments as they both entangle and come into being. This contribution also aims to nuance and broaden a branch of creative anthropological knowledge production by experimenting with analytical and textual compositions that allow us to attune and adjust our analytical perspectives to grasp the sounds, tones, sensations and affects of unnoticed events that come to matter to the people involved. We argue that this kind of attention and attunement to empirical details creates special entry points and access to empirical worlds, making other analytical and epistemological processes possible. In this regard, the anthology is also a tiny manifesto applauding the significance of detail- and material-oriented ethnographic work.

In the following paragraphs we unfold our approach to define and study the field we understand as in-between phenomena, our pocket-ethnographical approach and attunement in writing.

Studying phenomena of the *in-between*

Across the chapters, the contributing authors engage with what we seek to understand as phenomena of the *in-between*. Although we apply a deliberately vague, preliminary and open definition, we understand the in-between as something that emerges in the flow of everyday life: in people's ordinary doings, in oft-repeated routines, or as a part of what is usually going on. Tim Ingold writes that "… correspondence is about the ways along which lives, in their perpetual unfolding or becoming, simultaneously join together and differentiate themselves, one from another" (2021, p. 9). In living, working and corresponding with the world as researchers, we participate in everyday life, we encounter routines of the familiar, patterns of the expected and the ordinary. Meanwhile, we also find ourselves in situations where ambiguity is at play – situations that are inexplicable, that call for our attention, seem to escape their context or to lack their footing or metaphorical hinges by not hanging on to anything definable. Such situations constitute small in-between cracks in everyday life because they challenge our understandings and expectations, or maybe just because they testify to a world that is fundamentally adrift, irrational, alive and becoming. These situations and phenomena find us, as we find them, in the mid-streams of everyday life (see Ingold 2015, p. 147-53). They materialize in-between established categories and distinctions, and in this sense they are interstices, openings into life's small unknowns where nothing is certain. As Ingold writes, "'In-between' (…) is a movement of generation and dissolution in a world of becoming where things are not yet given – such that they might be joined up – but on the way to being given" (2015, p. 147). Drawing on this notion, the anthology explores how such in-betweens come to matter in the lives of human beings, how they may occur, take shape, sometimes even inflict shape and direction, and how they can be pockets charged with indecisive energies, vitality and sensations. In this sense, the in-between is not an empty space, not a vacuum, not a void, and not an isolated moment in time. On the contrary, the in-between occurs in the flow of ordinary life and emerges either unexpected, as a 'by-product' of more definable doings, or when people intentionally attach and hold on to each other and/or to the things and elements in their surroundings. Thus, focusing on the in-between is a way to address the sensations that arise in certain moments, and to grasp the quality of everyday entanglement as it bears significance and particular meaning to people in everyday situations. In this regard, the chapters unfold and engage with small moments, events and happenings experienced in our ethnographic fields in order to develop alternative analytical approaches to ordinary and taken-for-granted aspects of everyday life.

'Pocket-ethnography' as a generative metaphor

Embedded in the practice of writing ethnography is a tradition of explicit methodological awareness centred on the general characteristics of qualitative empirical knowledge production, such as scientific ethics and representational issues. Meanwhile, these concerns are not the aim of this volume and, due to the focus outlined above, methodological reflections are either entirely absent or discreet and kept to a minimum. Instead of dwelling on the (meta-)conditions of our research, we have dedicated this book to the exposition of empirically based findings and phenomena as they materialize during fieldwork, as they emerge in the midst of analytical processes, or as they render themselves unavoidable, powerful and increasingly decisive somewhere along the bumpy and crooked paths towards recognition. To frame this interest, we employ the generative metaphor of *pocket-ethnography*, a notion that is outlined in the following paragraphs.

Firstly, 'the pocket' is synonymous with the small crack, the in-between crevice or cleft that may potentially offer adventure if ventured into (e.g. Stewart 2012). In our fieldwork and interpretations of our empirical material, pockets are small moments where something demands our attention even though almost nothing seems to happen (cf. Ehn & Löfgren 2010). As such, we do not see pockets as demarcated or well-defined parts of our empirical material, but more as details or micro-elements in larger bundles of empirical experience that function as potential starting points for analytical awareness, curiosity and exploration. Conducting pocket-ethnography means dwelling on aspects which, at first sight, might not seem to have a significant impact on the practices observed.

Secondly, 'the pocket' is a soft compartment characteristic of jackets, jeans and other clothing. The pocket invites a collection of small items and everyday stuff; elements that, almost unnoticed, gather, meet and merge in the dark. In pockets we encounter lint comprised of various remnants that occupy these small and dark spaces of our garment: an old concert ticket almost unrecognizable due to weeks of continuous tumble, grains of sand, small stones, a crumpled receipt and the fluffy compositions of worn out cotton fibres, fine particles of tissue and dust. In the pocket we find distilled works of everyday life. Lint is the definition of 'nothing'; it has the indefinable form and feel of 'nothing' or 'almost nothing', and yet it is an exemplary product of everyday life and practice. These remains are what we find when we turn our pockets inside out; a substance of apparent nothingness and simultaneously a product of everyday life created and refined in the practice of everyday life. Meanwhile, this indeterminate substance of lint is also highly potent, sometimes allowing us to connect with a range of phenomena and experiences through sensory contact. Stories, reflections of lived life, sensations and memories entangle in these remnants and, as we fumble in our pockets, potent sparks and sensations can hit us with a sudden force. As when touched emotionally by the discovery of old artefacts and photographs in the darkness of an attic, or when hit by the atmospheres residing in the nooks and crannies of places that are important to us (cf. Bachelard 1994; Winther in this volume), sensations, charges and sparks also emanate from 'pockets', whether these are understood literally or used as a metaphor in the sense outlined above.

Studying what we define as the in-between events in the flow of everyday life with a pocket-ethnographical approach calls for new analytical experiments and foci – they crave different kinds of magnifying glasses and lenses. Working around the generative metaphor and notion of pocket-ethnography enables us to describe and frame the interest shared by the contributing authors. Each in our own way, we are all preoccupied with this 'delving into the darkness' in search of lint-like and potent phenomena. We are engaged in the analytical amplification of everyday 'nothingness' – the stuff found in-between – while agreeing on the sheer power contained in the depths of our metaphorical pockets. Meanwhile, we do not intend to develop a shared theoretical approach. Rather, the analytical endeavour of the chapters is to develop particular and empirically sensitive approaches that can amplify and bring forth the character of in-betweenness. In this regard, pocket-ethnography is synonymous with a certain style of ethnographic inquiry and with a desire to carry out research defined by openness, persistence and experimentation.

Analytical attunement in writing

Working with pocket-ethnography also requires what we define as an *analytical attunement* in writing. In a text on 'imaginative writing', the ethnographer Denielle Elliott asks the elementary and ever-important question "How do we write ethnography?" (2017, p. 24). She proceeds with two further questions that are also highly relevant in the context of this book: "What sorts of things do we pay attention to in our writing? What sorts of things do we deliberately leave out?" (ibid.). Elliott distinguishes between *form,* writing in an imaginative way, and *content,* writing about ideas that engage the imagination (ibid.). In this dualistic framing, ethnographic experimentation is either about words and linguistic-literary practice or about unfolding imaginative and creative analyses in an academically familiar and established prose. The contributions in this book challenge such conformal views of analytical ethnographic practice. Instead, we regard ethnographic writing as a process of paying attention. Through writing, we gain new possibilities of focus and scale as the composition of text offers opportunities for displacement and a dislocation of perspectives (e.g. Mogensen & Rasmussen 2017). Put differently, writing always carries transformative potentials (see Stewart 2015). In this book, we work with these potentials, both in the form of the applied focus on empirical knowledge and of imaginative and experimental writing. What has been called 'creative anthropology' (e.g. Lavie, Narayan & Rosaldo 1993) is a central ambition and a necessity in the development of pocket-ethnographic work. Whereas creativity is a general prerequisite for any anthropological analysis, the pocket-ethnographical endeavour is characterized by close attention to small everyday cracks and an interest in exposing them in writing. With a pocket-ethnographic approach, we take different theoretical points of departure, composing slightly odd or 'off-kilter' analytical perspectives that are able to produce new and different knowledge concerning phenomena that have already been described within the field of social studies: the city, school life, motherhood, leisure activities, inhabiting houses and bodies. The analytical work shows how daily life is imbued with myriad small-scale events, meanings and connections, many of which are surprisingly significant once we take a closer look. Pocket-ethnography is defined by exactly this ambition – taking a closer look. What we strengthen and qualify here is knowledge of affective dimensions in everyday life. Furthermore, we argue that it is productive to break or bend the rules and expectations inherent to academic writing, both in terms of knowledge production and acquisition and of analytical development. Adopting this point, we stand on the shoulders of a number of ethnographers and writers who have already demonstrated the wonderful potentials of such experimentation (Berlant & Stewart 2019; Desjarlais 2019; Kusserow 2017; Pandian & McLean 2017; Rosaldo 2014; Stevenson 2017; Taussig 2011, 2015; Tsing 2015).

A walk-through of the book's chapters

The seven chapters in this anthology take different approaches towards understanding the tight-knit connections and relations between human beings and the places in which they live and reside. A number of chapters focus on the meaning of senses, sounds, materials and environment. What stories, meanings, and cultural norms are embedded in certain materials, practices and particular buildings? How do people engage with faraway worlds, actualities, stories, pasts and presents when they interact with material stuff, dwell and immerse themselves in their surroundings? Some chapters show how socio-material environments affect everyday life and the authors develop analyses that focus on classrooms, skate parks, street corners, a sandpit, and specific objects, such as a football, a metal stick and a bench, and on the ability of these things to entangle with people and create moments, cracks and everyday situations charged with meanings and possibilities. It is analysed how different forms of matter influence school life, street life, and how staged activities create the potential to alter lifeworlds in a broader perspective. The chapters all deal with bodies, proximities, material and corporeal expressions that occur in the contexts and among the people studied. The ethnographer is included in a number of the texts, either as a participant observer or as the catalyst around which the writing circles. Furthermore, the empirical findings are presented and disseminated by drawing on different genres and approaches to writing. A couple of the contributions also experiment with the very object of ethnographic inquiry – not for the sake of experimentation alone, but because the unnoticed phenomena explored call for slightly alternative formats, for analytical and/or linguistic twists.

Following this introductory chapter, the book contains six empirically based chapters and an epilogue. In the section below, we briefly introduce the different chapters, outline their particular contributions and show how each chapter fits within the common framework of the anthology.

Drawing on a critique of mainstream individualism, Naja Dahlstrup Mogensen explores her experiences of pregnancy and becoming a mother in her chapter entitled *The hand in the mouth: Stories from a shared body*. In the text, she (Mogensen) develops an empirical figure called *the hand in the mouth* and through this figure explores how becoming and being in the world can be understood as a social-existential and spatial body practice. *The hand* in the figure is her son's while *the mouth* is Naja's, and her analysis grows out of several scenes in which this empirical figure took place during her maternity leave. The empirical material consists primarily of field notes characterized by a radical first-person perspective and literary devices. *The hand in the mouth* touches upon culturally embedded ideas of what it means to be a human being, including the idea, and critique, of autonomous individuals. Thus, the highly personal material and the style in which the chapter is written lead – through the analysis – to an understanding of *the hand in the mouth* as an in-between figure that insists on we-ness. Furthermore, it enables a contribution to a concept of social existence and the body as a place where we are always more than one.

This is followed by Nanna Jordt Jørgensen's chapter entitled *Sensations of sand and place* in which she explores sand as a connecting force involved in making place and politics of place among children and adults in a context of Danish day-care institutions. Ethnographically studying the particularities of children's everyday play in sandpits, Jørgensen discusses how sand as a material is sensed and made to make sense in relation to place in processes where children, adults, sand, playground and notions of childhood and community entangle and connect. With attention to the migration experiences of refugee children and parents in Denmark, the chapter explores how sand makes connections to home and to the past, how the place and boundaries of sand are negotiated in playgrounds, and how sand plays a role in creating a sense of belonging, as well as non-belonging, in relation to the day-care institution and to the nation state.

In *Attunement to school and classmates,* Karen Ida Dannesboe explores the ways in which children attune to school and each other in everyday school life. Based on an ethnographic study of children's school lives, Dannesboe follows bodily and social engagement in the small and often unnoticed events that emerge within ordinary school life as small cracks in the teacher-organized activities and the school's time structure. Zooming in on the entanglements of school materialities, children's personal belongings, children's bodies and small everyday practices, the chapter discusses how such micro-processes in ordinary school life create kinds of attuned in-betweenness connecting children with each other and to school. Analysing ongoing processes of attunement to school, the chapter demonstrates how children are affected differently by past and present experiences that leave some children hanging at the margins of school while others have fragile connections to a school they perceive an alienating place.

Jon Dag Rasmussen's chapter *The companion city – an initial ramble* ventures into an exploration of the relations between elderly city inhabitants and the Danish capital, Copenhagen. Based on long-term ethnographic work, the chapter examines how the city is understood and experienced as a companion in the lives of those followed – all of whom lead most of their everyday lives in winding, unnoticed and mobile practices traversing the urban landscape. The chapter sets out to expose the ambiguous and changeable relationships between particular elderly people and the city as an omnipresent *creature* – an experienced superorganism, a companion and a withdrawn, albeit ever-present and perceived, friend. The text is crafted in an experimental style of writing that includes various elements of empirical, theoretical and poetic heritage. This kind of *alchemical writing* is an integral part of the effort to grasp an ephemeral and fuzzy phenomenon as it has emerged alongside particular elderly people in Copenhagen.

The next chapter, *Designing place through rhythms and affinities*, is by Anne-Lene Sand. Through ethnographic fieldwork, Sand participated in the event Street on Wheels in which wheelchair users were offered an opportunity to experiment in a regular skateboarding environment. Through sensory emplaced participation – by participating in a wheelchair herself – Sand was allowed to carry out design anthropological reflections concerning the specific setting and the frame that the event constructs. The experience enables her to analyse how a new 'social design frame' opens up an in-between space in which wheelchair users are given alternative possibilities, both individual and social. The chapter specifically illustrates underlying rhythms, sparks, flows and social energies within in-between dimensions that, even though they can be difficult to grasp, are important to our understanding of place. In a broader perspective, designing places for just a single day is interesting since it can facilitate a discussion about how places can be designed temporarily and create alternative sensory experiences and participatory spaces.

Ida Wentzel Winther's chapter *The house: being, seeing, remembering place*, is written in the form of a textual mosaic that extends beyond the classical academic text. In the chapter, Winther shows how memories of the house, past and present, are constituted in-between herself as a writing and experiencing subject and the specific place. The jumping-off point is a red-brick house built in 1927, that Ida's family has lived in and occupied across four generations. The house, its landscapes and environment are imbued with myriad sensations, experiences and memories and the chapter addresses how memory finds its place, how it takes place, and how places are remembered and constructed in curious entanglements of sensory stimulus, bodily presence, material and immaterial kinds of belonging. Winther moves between layers of personal, familial, local and historical knowledge and details as well as the sensations arising throughout the narrative relate to her own embodied knowledge. Perhaps, the author asks, we carry 'the grammar of place' within us as a grid of experiences acquired, lived and stored through generations?

The book concludes with an epilogue by the Swedish ethnologist and distinguished scholar of everyday life Orvar Löfgren. In his text, Löfgren relates his own extensive studies and insights to the book's chapters and the scientific landscape they plot. Löfgren's text summarizes the anthology's overall contribution while offering important perspectives in its own right. Employing the notion of pocket-ethnography developed in this chapter, Löfgren presents a series of perceptive empirical descriptions and analyses concerning the phenomenon of everyday mornings. By unfolding a number of in-between elements inherent to morning routines, rituals, situations and dramas, the potentials of exploring the unnoticed cracks of everyday life are further qualified and expanded. With this concluding contribution, it is emphasized how the study of seemingly small and unnoticed aspects can reveal surprisingly powerful insights into the domains of everyday life.

References

Bachelard, G. (1994 [1958]). *The Poetics of Space*. Boston: Beacon Press.

Bech-Jørgensen, B. (1994). *Når hver dag bliver hverdag*. Copenhagen: Akademisk Forlag.

Benjamin, W. (2003). *The Arcades Project*. Cambridge: Harvard University Press.

Benjamin, W. (2006). *Berlin Childhood Around 1900*. Cambridge: Belknap Press of Harvard University Press.

Berlant, L. & Stewart, K. (2019). *The Hundreds*. Durham: Duke University Press.

Carlson, J. D. & Stewart, K. C. (2014). The legibilities of mood work. *New Formations*, 114-33.

de Certeau, M.(1984). *The Practice of Everyday Life*. University of California Press.

Desjarlais, R. R. (2019). *The Blind Man: A Phantasmography*. New York: Fordham University Press.

Ehn, B. & Löfgren, O. (2010). *The Secret World of Doing Nothing*. University of California Press.

Ehn, B. & Löfgren, O. (2017). At analysere det oversete. In Andersen, P. T. & Jacobsen, M. H. (Eds.) *Kultursociologi og Kulturanalyse* (pp. 137-65). Copenhagen: Hans Reitzels Forlag.

Elliott, D. (2017). Writing. In Denielle Elliott & Dara Culhane (Eds.), *A Different Kind of Ethnography: Imaginative Practices and Creative Methodologies* (pp. 23-44). Toronto: University of Toronto Press.

Harvey, P. & Knox, H. (2014). Objects and materials: An introduction. In Harvey, Penny, Casella, Eleanor Conlin, Evans, Gillian, Knox, Hannah, McLean, Christine, Silva, Elizabeth B., Thoburn, Nicholas & Woodward, Kath (Eds.) *Object and Materials*. London: Routledge.

Highmore, B. (2011). *Everyday Life: Critical Concepts in Media and Cultural Studies*. London: Routledge.

Ingold, T. (2011). *Being Alive: Essays on Movement, Knowledge and Description*. London: Routledge.

Ingold, T. (2015). *The Life of Lines*. London: Routledge.

Ingold, T. (2021). *Correspondences*. Cambridge: Polity.

Lavie, S., Narayan, K. & Rosaldo, R. (Eds.) (1993). *Creativity/Anthropology*. Ithaca: Cornell University Press.

Jacobsen, M. Hviid (Ed.) (2009). *Encountering the Everyday: An Introduction to the sociologies of the unnoticed*. Basingstoke: Palgrave Macmillan.

Kusserow, A. (2017). Anthropoetry. In Anand Pandian & Stuart McLean (Eds.), *Crumpled Paper Boat: Experiments in Ethnographic Writing* (pp. 71-90). Durham: Duke University Press.

Lefevbre, H. (1991). *The Production of Space*. Malden, Mass: Blackwell.

Manning, E. (2016). *The Minor Gesture*. Durham: Duke University press.

Mason, J. (2018). *Affinities – Potent Connections in Personal Life*. Cambridge: Polity.

Mogensen, N. Dahlstrup & Rasmussen, J. D. (2017). (I og om) Fletværk: Nogle foreløbige viklinger. *Tidsskriftet Antropologi*, 76, pp. 13-35.

Pandian, A. & McLean, S. (Eds.) (2017). *Crumpled Paper Boat: Experiments in Ethnographic Writing*. Durham: Duke University Press.

Perec, G. (2008 [1974]). *Species of Spaces and Other Pieces*. New York: Penguin Classics.

Rosaldo, R. (2014). Notes on poetry and ethnography. In *The Day of Shelly's Death: The Poetry and Ethnography of Grief* (pp. 101-13). Durham: Duke University Press.

Schroer, S. A. & Schmitt, S. B. (2018). *Exploring Atmospheres Ethnographically*. Oxon: Routledge.

Stewart, K. (2007). *Ordinary Affects*. Durham: Duke University Press.

Stewart, K. (2012). Pockets. *Communication and Critical/Cultural Studies*, 9(4), 365-68.

Stewart, K. (2015). New England Red. In Vannini, Phillip (Ed.), *Non-representational Methodologies: Re-envisioning Research* (pp. 19-33). New York: Routledge.

Taussig, M. (2015). *The Corn Wolf*. Chicago: University of Chicago Press.

Taussig, M. (2011). *I swear I saw This: Drawings in Fieldwork Notebooks, Namely my Own*. Chicago: University of Chicago Press.

Tsing, A. L. (2015). *The Mushroom at the End of the World: On the Possibility of Life in Capitalist Ruins*. Princeton: Princeton University Press.

CHAPTER 2:

'The hand in the mouth': stories from a shared body

Naja Dahlstrup Mogensen

There. It is here again. The hand. I know it's coming, but I am still surprised every time. It finds its way up, up to me, up to the mouth, from you down there. You are at the breast, nursing, you are lying there. The hand finds its way up, you latch onto me. You are falling asleep, you fall asleep, you wake up again, dash around inside my mouth, you scratch, on the teeth, the gums, the palate, scratch my lip, and here comes all of the hand, a clenched fist that drills itself into my mouth, I open my mouth, and now the fingers spread themselves, you come too far inside, I can feel my gag reflex, draw the head backwards, you fumble feverish in the air, find the mouth again – one more time! The fingers live, they look, they are up to something, they want something, what is it you want?

(fieldnote)

Introducing the text

In this chapter, I want to explore the hand in the mouth at play in the above fieldnote. The hand is my son's, the mouth is mine, and the scene in the fieldnote is one of many, in which my son's hand found my mouth numerous times a day during a period of around 6 months – in such an insistent way and with so much intensity that it has called, if not screamed, to be examined. In this way, 'the hand in the mouth' can be understood as *a potent connection* (Mason 2018). Mason suggests that taking such connections "seriously and exploring them opens up new and exciting possibilities for conceptualising living in the world" (Mason 2018, p. 1). This text both is the result of and represents in itself such an exploration. In this exploration, I shall work with and call this potent connection an *empirical figure*. Here, *figure* does not refer to numbers, or any kind of generalised type or pattern, but is used as a visual concept, cf. figurative art. Thus, figure in this case points to concreteness, materiality and body – a hand in a mouth. It is synonymous with the notion of *image*, which – together with stories, scenes, sounds and senses – is foregrounded in Arts-Based Research (ABR), as opposed to numbers in quantitative research and words in qualitative research (Leavy 2009, p. 256). I shall return to ABR later. The adverb *empirical*, supporting the notion of the figure, stresses the fact that this particular figure is based on empirical experience. The empirical material explored in this text is not produced during fieldwork far away from home; on the contrary, it takes place at home and in what we can think of as the most private space: the bedroom. Moreover, it is produced in a period that we tend to perceive as some sort of dead time in our work life, namely maternity leave. In that way, the paper takes a feministic standpoint; the private (space and time) is not only political but can also be highly scientifically relevant, and it is an example of the kind of cultural analysis that is occupied with the overlooked and seemingly irrelevant: "phenomena that do not let themselves define in well-established categories, but live in in-between spaces and cracks, are put in the shade and become insignificant, irrational or contradictory – becoming a kind of culture analytical left-over categories" (Ehn & Löfgren 2017, p. 161f, my translation). As a visual concept, the empirical figure implies, of course, that someone is seeing. That someone is me. I am the one who decides to make this cut – as a result of my research interests, my embodied experiences, and what I like to call embodied theory. No production of empirical material is theory-free, since it is produced by a researcher body, and thus the distinction between empirical material, theory and analysis is not as sharp as we often like to think. The empirical figure, being a synthesis of empirical experience and analytical gaze, places itself in-between empirical knowledge and analysis – in a scientific crack. This text experiments with that crack by zooming in on an intimate space between two people, a son and his mother, the latter also being a social scientist and a writer of both poetry and ethnography.

An arts-based autoethnography

Right from the first line in the fieldnote above, there is an I at play. This I is an *ethnographic I*, which plays a central role in the text; it is a very clear I, which is connected to the mouth in the scene. It is an experiencing I, and an I that also addresses a you, which plays the second leading part in the text, and which is connected to the hand. The I is also an *autoethnographic I;* It is I – the person also writing this chapter – who has chosen to write a text on the basis of personal experiences with this particular empirical phenomenon. In that way, this text is also a piece of autoethnography.

> *Autoethnography is an approach to research and writing that seeks to describe and systematically analyse* (graphy) *personal experience* (auto) *in order to understand cultural experience* (ethno) (Ellis et al. 2011, p. 1).

I do not understand autoethnography as something spectacular or essentially different from other ethnography but rather as an intensification of something intrinsically ethnographic: "the ethnographic enterprise is always, in some degree, autoethnographic in that the ethnographer's self is always implicated in the research process" (Atkinson 2006, p. 403). The ethnographer always filters the world, but this filtration becomes more evident when the text operates with a radical first-person perspective. The purpose, however, is the same as for every other ethnography: namely, analysis and development of anthropologically relevant concepts. In order to benefit scientifically from the manifold everyday resources that the I has access to, working autoethnographically involves 1) an obligation to bring the everyday experiences out of the everyday and into an analytical process, which contributes to a theoretical understanding of broader social phenomena (Anderson 2006), and 2) an awareness of the scope of the autoethnographic work. Accepting that it is impossible to describe and document a problem in its entirety, Mason develops *facet methodology* "as an orientation and an approach, rather than a set of procedures that can be encapsulated in a framework or a recipe for research. As an orientation, it requires and celebrates researcher creativity, inventiveness, a 'playful' approach to epistemology, and the pursuit of 'flashes of insight' (Mason 2011, p. 76). I understand and explore the hand in the mouth as a way to elicit such a flash of insight. Allowing myself to pursue this potential flash of insight as a small, seemingly irrelevant practice from the everyday life of maternity leave, and at the same time allowing the text to be experimental, can thus be seen as a way of working in accordance with the orientation of facet methodology. As such, with both the choice of content and the form of the text, I explore the potentialities of a certain kind of autoethnography (in)formed by Arts-Based Research (Leavy 2018) – an *arts-based autoethnography* with special focus on *poetic inquiry* (Faulkner 2018):

> *As an ABR method, autoethnography is invested in connecting researchers, participants, and readers/audiences not only with the intellectual and knowledge-based aspects of the self ↔ culture dance, but also, and just as importantly, with the emotional, sensory, and embodied experience of social life* (Adams & Jones 2018, p. 146).

> *Poetry constitutes a way to say things evocatively and to say things that may not be presented at all* (Faulkner 2018, p. 221).

> *Poetry in research is a way to tap into universality and radical subjectivity* (Faulkner 2018, p. 210).

In some way, this chapter combines (primarily) two very different types of text, namely the fieldnotes and the analysis thereof. *The fieldnotes* express the first-person perspective of a mother's experience with her son's hand movements during the child's breastfeeding and falling asleep. The fieldnotes are characterised by a radical first-person perspective and literary devices. I insist on calling them fieldnotes (and thereby hopefully contributing to an expansion of the genre), since they are notes from the field of human being and becoming – written exactly like most other fieldnotes: the first lines scrawled down in the field (on my phone in the notes app, sitting in our bed, nursing, with my son's hand in my mouth) and later the same day expanded on my computer. They are not thick descriptions, however, but poetic enquiries. The language is very spontaneous; through my fingers, the words found their own way out of my experiencing body, and they have not been edited. It is important, however, to stress that these unedited stories are not neutral material. The conceptual work of this chapter already begins in the writing of the fieldnotes, hence the blurred distinctions between empirical material, theory and analysis. In this way, ethnographic texts must be understood as crafted, developing concepts by writing through the material in different ways. *The analysis* can be understood as a text analysis of the fieldnotes, carried out in order to follow where the fieldnotes might lead and to place the particular experience in a wider social context. This part of the text is characterised by a more conventional academic writer's distance. Writing the analysis, I felt a strong impulse to distance myself from the fieldnotes and look at them as if they were not written by me. This happened quite unconsciously at first, but in hindsight I can see two main reasons for this. One reason is a need to counterbalance the very personal fieldnotes and the highly intimate subject expressed in them – a need that resembles Wyatt's use of third-person voice as a way to create "a fitting psychic distance" while writing about his father's death. He describes how writing in the first person "brought the readers in too close" (Wyatt as cited in Adams & Jones 2018, p. 150). The other reason is my general analytical style, which is formed by my background in literature, and with which I tend to access fieldnotes as literary texts – unfolding bigger stories from the smallest of words. In this case, where the fieldnotes have lyrical qualities, this analytical strategy seems to fit quite well, but the distant (text) analytical approach differs from a lot of autoethnography, which does not usually operate with these two very different types of text. This is why I categorise this particular autoethnography as an arts-based autoethnography occupied with poetic enquiry. Thus, in this chapter, I work on two levels distinguished by two interlinked but very different kinds of writing. By doing so, I exploit and explore the distinction that is made when a poem has left the writing body, and which resonates with the beautiful words of biographer Susan Howe (as cited in Adams & Jones 2018, p. 160):

What I put into words is no longer my possession. Possibility has opened. The future will forget, erase or recollect.

Following this line of thought, the analysis presented in this chapter can be understood as a recollection. Taking that thought a step further, the scientific paper in general can be thought of as a memory, each paper reminding us of something different. Thus, by claiming scientific space for this particular kind of experience or everyday life crack, this specific chapter responds to what philosopher Peter Sloterdijk (2014) has called *an oblivion of birth*, by reminding us that we have all inhabited someone else's body.

On the way into this recollective analysis, I would like to point out some other central notions in this text, introduced in the first fieldnote. In addition to the I, there is also a you, which on an empirical level is my son, during a period spanning 9 to 15 months old, and which on an analytical level contributes to the text with a second person perspective; in the fieldnotes, I don't write *about* the child, but *address* the child directly. In the fieldnote, I am the 'I' relating to a 'you' in a very intimate relationship. On the analytical level, however, I shall also write about the child in a third-person perspective, just like I shall refer to myself as *the mother* or *the I*. This use of third-person perspective correlates with the distance explained above in relation to the two types of text. It might be helpful to conceive of this distinction through an analogy to a painting and looking at a painting. It is like this: I painted a painting and afterwards looked at it in order to see what it could tell me. In the painting, *I am the mother*, while looking at it, *I see a mother* (who is both a mother and an I). This is not simple, and I move in and out of these positions (between particular first-person perspectives and general third-person perspectives), but as mentioned above, this text is an experimenting exploration of what this kind of work can look like and lead to.

As a result of the particular textual constellation, the fieldnotes (being spontaneous poetic expressions and not thick descriptions) imply knowledge about the child, which I (as the mother) have because I have spent every single minute with him, but which I do not explain further. For instance, in a subsequent fieldnote, I write about my son's fear of falling asleep. I do not explain or make this fear probable, and therefore it can look like a postulate. But (the causal question of) *why* my son is afraid of falling asleep is not the interest here; my interest is *what* he does with his hand and *how* he does it, in a situation where he is afraid of falling asleep, creating a very intimate and shared space between two bodies. And my access to this goes through the first-person perspective as the receiving part of this act – me as another human being and a mother. Thus, resting on arts-based and not classical ethnographic fieldnotes, the text is somehow asking for some other degree of trust from the reader. There is fear because the (arts-based, autoethnographically working) mother writes about fear; fear is part of the picture, whether the child is 'really' afraid or not. The you is there through the I. I don't have access to the child's first-person perspective, which however exists and – in a phenomenological perspective – should not be neglected. The first-person perspective is connected to me, and the fieldnotes express my experience of the empirical phenomenon.

Moving along, the opening fieldnote points towards a pivotal theme in this text, to which I shall return later, namely *the body*. In addition to the breastfeeding that sets the scene above (where the *you* is at the breast, nursing), the importance of the body is seen through the attention that is given to the two parts of the empirical figure in the fieldnote: the mouth is described in its constituent parts (for instance teeth, gums, palate, lip) and with synonyms (for instance jaws), while the hand is the active part, which *comes, finds its way, dashes around, tears, drills itself into*, becomes fingers that *spread themselves, come too far inside, fumble, live and look*. Moreover, all the above mentioned verbs point towards how much movement the nursing situation entails; it's just full speed ahead, and the verbs often come with adverbials of place and direction which both underlines the movement dimension and points towards the specific connection established between the I and the you through 'the hand in the mouth': the hand *finds its way* <u>up</u>, <u>up to me</u>, <u>up to the mouth, from you</u> <u>down there</u>, while the fingers at some point come <u>too far inside</u> and the head is drawn <u>backwards</u>. The intensity and character of the movements of the hand would differ from time to time; sometimes the hand would fight as if its life depended on it, sometimes it was fervently exploring, and sometimes it was as if it fell into place; *There you go! Here; this is where I was going.* However, regardless of intensity and character, I always experienced the hand as alive and active, and this is also how the fieldnote ends – with a question pointing towards an idea of an intention, or at least a search for some kind of meaning: "The fingers live, they look, they are up to something, they want something", and in the last part the I addresses the you directly, in wonder: "What is it you want?" That is the question that drives me into analysis.

Clinging to the world

> *Your hand rests on the neckline, it hangs there, attached. You hold on tight, make a sudden movement, you are falling – off the world? – but you get a hold of the blouse, you are still here, you are not gone, we take care of that, you and I, you attach yourself and I offer a hook, I am a hook, you are a hook, we are going nowhere now, we are sitting here, time has stopped and yet you have left, into the sleep that you fear but are learning to fall into,*
>
> *we teach each other everything,*
> *we are each other's everything,*
> *we are each other,*
> *we are,*
> *we*
> *are*

(fieldnote)

Alongside nursing, *the hand in the mouth* unfolds especially in connection with sleep – or, more accurately, in connection with the movement that we have also built into the language when we say that we *fall* asleep. The situation described in the fieldnote takes place right after the child *has* fallen asleep; calmness has found its way into the hand, which has found its way out of the mouth and now rests on the neckline of the blouse; the hand has fallen from mouth to blouse as the child has fallen asleep. But it still clings; it has not completely surrendered yet. Thus, the child starts (*[you] make a sudden movement*) in the fieldnote as if it was momentarily free falling (*you are falling – off the world?*) before attaching itself once again (*but you get a hold of the blouse*). And that is the central and dominant motif in this fieldnote: *to attach* – a motif which is also found in the similar expression *to hold on tight*. Along with the other accompanying expressions about the hand that *rests on* the neckline, *it hangs there*, and the fact that it *gets a hold of*, in the fieldnote *the attachment* appears as the antithesis to the *fall* implied in the sleeping, and which is furthermore somehow connected to some kind of threat: the sleeping which the you – according to the I – fears. Thus, we are also introduced to something difficult. This is not the iconic safe and harmoniously sleeping baby who can barely be woken up (cf. the expression *s/he sleeps like a baby*), but a startling child who calms down *through* attachment. Once again, the fieldnote is filled with movement – the antithesis to the picture of a sleeping baby where everything stands still. *Time has stopped*, it says in the middle of the fieldnote, so this dimension is also part of this picture – but it is surrounded by movement: the startling child has left, into the sleep, in which way it is both present and gone at the same time. Where do we go when we sleep? I neither can nor shall answer that question here, but there is clearly both a *here* and a *there* at play in this fieldnote: *you are still <u>here</u>, you are not gone; we are going nowhere now, we are sitting <u>here</u>*. This *here* is a concrete and recognizable place, tied to a familiar materiality in the form of the blouse (which is repeated throughout the fieldnote). Furthermore, this *here* is contrasted with *a diffuse other place*, which is expressed in different ways in the fieldnote as 1) the sleep as somewhere else, 2) an abstract *gone* and 3) an undefined place at the edge of the world; *off the world*. The concrete *here* and the abstract *there* are present at the same time, like for instance in the sentence "You are falling – off the world? – but you get a hold of the blouse". The abstract world and the concrete blouse appear close. Thus, in this note, *here* and *there* are present at the same time – and at the same place, one could say. Furthermore, the diffuse *there* is connected to the *you* and takes the shape of some kind of threat: "<u>you</u> are falling – <u>off the world</u>?", "<u>you</u> are not <u>gone</u>", and "yet <u>you</u> have left, into <u>the sleep</u> that <u>you fear</u> but are learning to fall into", while *here*, on the contrary, is a shared place; it is populated by a *we*; this is where *you* and *I* are together; "we are going nowhere now, we are sitting here". The first-person experience of a *we* expressed in the fieldnote here is established through the central motif about attaching which can be seen as the underlying motif in the figure *the hand in the mouth*. By attaching itself, the you works against the movement that would otherwise tear it away, *off the world*. And it does so by the physical (re)production of a shared body.

According to anthropologist Tim Ingold, *clinging* is an existential movement: "We have to cling to things, hoping that the friction of our contact will somehow suffice to countervail the currents that would otherwise sweep us to oblivion" (Ingold 2015, p. 3). This quote contains exactly the two conflicting movements above, which can be described as *disappearing* versus *clinging*. Thus, when the *I* in the opening fieldnote asks the final question, "What is it you want?", the answer from the child, the *you* in the note will, according to Ingold, be, "I want to cling!";

> *As infants, clinging is the first thing we ever did. Is not the strength in the new-born's hands and fingers remarkable? They are designed to cling, first to the little one's mother, then to others in its entourage, still later to the sorts of things that enable the infant to get around or to pull itself upright. But grown-ups cling too – to their infants, of course, lest they be lost, but also to one another for security, or in expressions of love and tenderness. And they cling to things that offer some semblance of stability. Indeed there would be good grounds for supposing that in clinging – or, more prosaically, in holding on to one another – lies the very essence of sociality* (Ingold 2015, p. 3).

Here, Ingold points out that the first thing we do as human beings coming into the world is clinging. Thus, clinging is this fundamental movement which Ingold also describes as "the very essence of sociality", exactly because it is a social act. The combination of the fundamental movements of existence and the fundamental sociality of this movement leads me to think of *clinging as a notion of social existence*. As Ingold points out, the great need of clinging does not disappear when we get older; grown-ups cling to their children, each other and things – out of love and for stability – in order to secure their existence, or, with reference to the fieldnote and the quote above, in order not to disappear. Thus, clinging and the we-ness it entails, work against the threat of not being here, expressed by Ingold above. And this is not something we can take care of by ourselves – in this movement, we need each other; the fieldnote above ends with a little "textual reduction" (*we teach each other everything* etc.), where every line begins with a *we*, that becomes essential. By deleting everything else but the first word in this little text, a *we-pillar* emerges:

we ~~*teach each other everything*~~,	*we*
we ~~*are each other's everything*~~,	*we*
we ~~*are each other*~~,	*we*
we ~~*are*~~,	*we*
we	*we*
are	*are*

The we-pillar can be understood as an insistence on sociality, and at the bottom of the pillar it flows into the first-person plural present tense of the fundamental existential verb of *being*, namely *are*. Thus, the *we* is gone in the very last sentence; however, as a result of the repetition, the *we* lives in the existential verb, and, in this way, the repetitive reduction text can be seen as a textual way of underlining the sociality of existence.

An interesting parallel appears here between the insisting language of the *we*-pillar and the insistence with which *the hand in the mouth* keeps returning (during one situation, like in the first fieldnote, and over time respectively) – a parallel which points back to the introductory methodological reflections on what kind of text this is and, moreover, what the potentiality of this poetic inquiring type of fieldnote can be. The analytical text is a process which leads to a new understanding of *the hand in the mouth*. Through the parallel between the insisting return of the hand and the insisting return of the *we* in the fieldnote, I come to work with the hand in the mouth as *an insistence on we-ness*. It is as if the *you* elaborates on the first and short answer from above, *I want to cling*, with an *I do not want to disappear, I want to be here, connect myself with you and thus exist. I cannot do that on my own, so please do not let me go!* Of course, the *you* does not speak! The child does not have a verbal language (yet), which means that I only have my own experience of the insistence of the hand to work with. Or, to be more accurate, I have my own experience *and* the experience expressed in language; my experience of the hand in the mouth, which keeps returning, is carried out in my language, and through analysis of my spontaneous language (= the fieldnote), I become aware of which kind of meaning can be drawn from my spontaneous experience. In that way, I approach my experience analytically.

This also says something about the status and character of the fieldnote. The fieldnote does not represent the field; its ambition is not to come close to a 1:1 representation; it is something else. By writing the fieldnote, I already fill (the sign) *the hand in the mouth* with meaning – by transforming the experience into language. But I also keep it open, partly by asking: *What is going on here? What does this mean?*, partly through the style of the fieldnote, which allows for literary devices and through that meaning beyond causality. The fieldnote leaves something open – an opening in language, which allows for another analytical movement: an analytical opening?

Ingold offers a good grip on the clinging itself, while Sloterdijk more thoroughly describes the circumstances that cause the need for clinging. In brief, with Sloterdijk (1989, p. 111), one could say that the condition that causes the need for clinging is that we are born – and through birth we are brought out into the open, boundless and insecure. These conditions cause what Sloterdijk calls *Anheftung* (fixation), which bears a certain similarity to Ingold's *clinging*. Because of birth, a certain fixation/binding is loosened, namely the one that tied mother and child together in uterine symbiosis, and, in the moment that this fetal community dissolves, the need for other ways to fix arise (Sloterdijk 1989, p. 109-10). The hand in the mouth can be seen as a very concrete expression for such a fixation, and in the fieldnote above it is expressed through the metaphor of the hook: "you attach yourself and I offer a hook, I am a hook, you are a hook". Ingold also uses the hook when he describes the hand as *the instrument of sociality*:

> *The linking of hands, palm to palm and with* **fingers bent to form a hook** [emphasis added], *does not here symbolise a togetherness that is attained by other means. Rather,* **hands are the means of togetherness** [emphasis added]. *That is, they are* **the instruments of sociality** [emphasis added], *which can function in the way they do precisely because of their capacity – quite literally – to interdigitate* (Ingold 2015, p. 6).

While Ingold's picture is about hands (in plural, 'palm to palm'), and thereby refers to some kind of equal reciprocity, the empirical figure *the hand in the mouth* only has one (singular) hand – in a mouth. Thus, as already described above, this particular relation is not a symmetrical relation; this picture is that of a baby son and his mother. The child is clinging to his mother, who meets his clinging by opening her mouth. At the same time, at least in the breastfeeding scenes, there *is* a kind of symmetry – when the nursing child also has the mother in his mouth. In every case, the clinging leads to the mother's experience of a strong and insisting we-ness.

Clinging is a central concept in Ingold's *linealogy* (2007, 2011, 2015) in which all life, human and non-human, is perceived as living lines. The linealogy is often criticized as abstract, and it can be hard to surrender to this idea of life as lines, which seem to lack flesh and blood – as opposed to the more massive *blobs*, with which we according to Ingold are in the habit of picturing living creatures – maybe exactly because the blob bears a more spontaneous resemblance with the bodies that we cannot renounce. The hand, however, offers an opportunity to put flesh on the bones of these lines (see photo below) when Ingold points to the hand not as a symbol but as an instrument. Hands are *the means of togetherness*, exactly the way the hand in the mouth is when it clings to the mouth. The hook is a metaphor, and as a metaphor it is based on *similarity* between literal and figurative levels, which in this case means that the hand, whose fingers bend to grip the mouth, can look *like* a hook. The hook is a good line figure because it bears a physical resemblance to the phenomenon and can look like a hand, and at the same time it can be converted to mere lines;

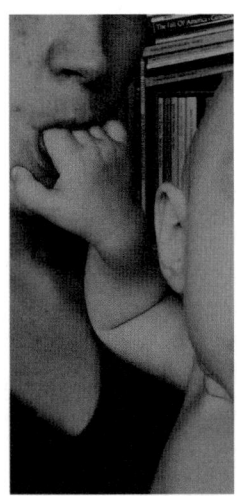
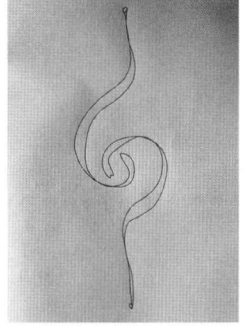

photo: the hand in the mouth   notebook drawing: two hooks

'The hand in the mouth': stories from a shared body

notebook drawing: line/s

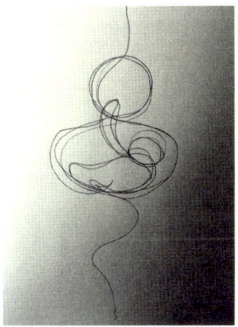

sketch: the hand in the mouth, mother and child, breastfeeding/nursing, line/s

The shared body

Today it is the feverish hand, yesterday it was the soft one, the warm soft child's hand, that finds its way home to my mouth, sending calmness out into the rest of the little body that becomes heavy. Quiet.

Fiddling, fiddling, fiddling, and then: quiet. You are asleep. I am sitting here. I am your mother. You have lived in here. In my body. The mass we call my body. You lived there. Now you are here. Outside. But still inside. You find your way home. Inside.

I wonder when you will become your own home. When is someone her own home? I only know that I have never felt more at home in my body than during the time when we were two living here.

(fieldnote)

37

Through the dominant outside-inside motif in this fieldnote, the body is connected with the theme of home: being at home and the body as a home. The note takes the form of a reflection made possible after the child has fallen asleep: *You are asleep. I am sitting here.* The partial disappearance into which sleep has carried the child leaves space for a reflection that takes the relation between the two as a starting point: *I am your mother.* It is followed by an elaboration of this relation, first in the past tense: *You have lived in here. In my body. The mass we call my body. You lived there.* And then in the present tense: *Now you are here. Outside. But still inside. You find your way home. Inside.* Thus, in this fieldnote there is a movement between inside and outside – in and out of a body that is the mother's (which is even referred to as both here and there). It all seems a bit messy – because it messes with our understanding of body limits. However, if one goes along with the language used, a striking order appears: *You have lived* **in there** *(…) Now you are here.* **Outside**. *But still* **inside**. This resembles the order of the three-act structure of fairy tales: home-out-home. Furthermore, the home also occurs as some kind of conclusion in the text: *You find your way home. Inside.* Thus, 'inside' and 'home' appear as synonyms, and they are connected to the mother. In this way, the body of the mother can be understood as a container (Winther 2006, p. 209f) in which the child has safely grown ready for the world, and which it is now learning to live outside. This learning process – like any other learning process – does not follow a straight line, but also involves backward movements; back into the body of the mother – through a path made possible by the mouth. However, this path has its boundaries; the child neither can nor shall go all the way back into the container. In the fieldnote, this is expressed in the last part, where the *I* in wonder, and maybe slightly impatient, first addresses the you directly, asking: *I wonder when* **you** *will become your own home.* This personal question is immediately rephrased into a generalised one: *When is* **someone** *her own home?* – before it is once again brought down to the personal, now as some kind of confession: *I only know that* **I** *have never felt more at home in my body than during the time when we were two living here.* In this way, the note contains the first-person experience of the *I*, a question to a second person, the *you*, and an imagined abstract third person, the general *someone*. And this is where we come close to the ambition of the analytical autoethnography – saying something about cultural phenomena on the basis of analysis of personal experience. In this connection, this fieldnote in particular, and 'the hand in the mouth' in general, touches upon certain cultural understandings of what it means to be a human being – not least a cultural story about autonomous individuals.

With Ingold (2015), the idea of the autonomous individual takes the form of the already mentioned *blob* that contrasts the line. Blobs are bounded units that can connect through straight lines (as visualised in many network analyses), but they cannot, however, achieve the proximity of the living lines of the linealogy as these entangle in temporary meshwork on their way through life. The idea of the autonomous individual can be found in the fieldnote through the dominant outside-inside terminology – exactly the distinction that Ingold finds to characterise the blob: "Blobs have insides and outsides, divided at their surface" (Ingold 2015, p. 3). However, as the analysis has shown, the *potent connection* of 'the hand in the mouth' transgresses the maintenance of two bounded blobs, and there is clearly a particular closeness at play in the empirical figure. 'The hand in the mouth' simply does not accept the surface of the blob. Thus, it questions the unity of body and person implicated in the idea of the autonomous individual, which is also at play in the fieldnotes – in particular in the mother's question about becoming one's own home, and in the general use of language, through the constant referring to *you* and *I*.

However, subjectivity is not necessarily tied to individuals. By zooming in on the fetal condition – the child's fetal communion with the mother – Sloterdijk defines subjectivity as something shared:

Der Humanraum ist (…) von Anfang an, buchstäblich ab utero, *zunächst bipolar, auf entwickelteren Stufen pluripolar geformt; er besitzt die Struktur und Dynamik eines – um altmodisch zu reden – beseelenden Ineinandergreifens von Lebewesen, die auf Nähe und Teilhabe aneinander angelegt sind* (Sloterdijk 2004, p. 14).

Closeness (*Nähe*) and participation (*Teilhabe*) are exactly what are at play with 'the hand in the mouth'; the two beings contributing to this figure are very close and take part in each other. They *are* part of each other! In the pregnant body, the *I* and the *you* are inseparable. But the child has been born now, it has a body and something we can call and recognise as a *you*. Nevertheless, it insists on the shared-ness, the part of each other-ness, the fundamental we-ness, when it momentarily crawls back into the body of the mother – through the mouth. This shared-ness is so fundamental that the *I* who undergoes the pregnant body experiences it as some kind of ideal condition – not because of some female nature, but because the pregnant body brings the matter to a head: we all began our lives as part of someone else, as part of a shared body.

In the fieldnote, the pregnancy is referred to as *the time when we were two living here*. The very last word, the spatial deixis *here*, refers to the body of the mother. This connection is at play throughout the entire fieldnote, and it leads me to think of the *body as a place* – and furthermore, in line with all of the above: *the body as a shared place*, which contrasts the body as an individual place. Such an idea resonates with knowledge from microbiology and bacteriology about "the fact that human genomes can be found in only about 10 percent of all the cells that occupy the mundane space I call my body; the other 90 percent of the cells are filled with the genomes of bacteria, fungi, protists, and such" (Haraway 2008, pp. 3-4).

I am not just *I*. We inhabit each other's bodies. Thus, contrasting a clean story about clear-cut autonomous individuals, this text tells a messy story about (some of) the complexity of shared bodies. The fieldnotes are written texts from a certain period in time, when the shared-ness was very explicit and insisting. However, a gathering of theory from anthropology, philosophy and microbiology points towards understanding the shared-ness of the *potent connection* of 'the hand in the mouth' as intensified rather than exceptional. Thus, the small stories from a specific shared body may tell a more general story about the shared-ness of bodies.

Through its insistence on the shared body, the empirical figure *the hand in the mouth* can be understood as an in-between figure that reminds us of the fundamental sociality of being-in-the-world. As such, the analysis of a mother's experience of the minor gesture (cf. Manning 2016 and the introductory chapter in this book) of her baby boy's hand is also a critique of the western idea of autonomous and well-defined individuals. Returning to the question of home posed in the latter fieldnote, it becomes relevant to ask if one ever becomes her own home. Through the first-person perspective to which the text offers access, readers gain insight into the cultural person who asks this question because she has learned along the way that you have to become your own home; you have to become yourself – *your self*. However, through the encounter with the hand in the mouth, the questions it evokes and the poetic fieldnotes it gives rise to, the same person is reminded of the fact that she herself has never felt more at home in her body than when she was not the only inhabitant – when she was not alone, but the home of someone else. Thus, she is reminded that being in the world is fundamentally social and that the initial question might well be the wrong one. A better question might be: *How* do we create a home? And the responding answer from the empirical figure would sound as follows: by clinging – and thereby creating shared places as we go along. Thus, home is created *with* others through social-existential experiences that happen in all kinds of seemingly irrelevant practices, in the cracks of everyday life.

The freedom of attention provided by autoethnography, to be aware of and follow potential flashes of insight in every aspect of life, including the personal, enables the researcher to access those spaces in-between that hide in the complexity of everyday life. I call this kind of attention free in that it is not limited to already accepted and well-defined research objects, but remains open to the smallest, most mundane and personal experiences. Through such an attention, I believe, the social sciences can find ways into spaces less studied – but nonetheless important. This chapter provides insight into a very intimate and shared space in-between two bodies. And it does so from and through analysis of a first-person perspective on the experience of being part of this shared body. It may seem like a paradox that the critique of the individual goes through a radical first-person perspective; however, only by zooming in on the particular experiences of the subject can the general sharedness of subjectivity become visible. Thus, the strong *I* and the strong *we* in this story do not reveal opposing ontologies; the pronoun *we* is plural and therefore implies exactly plurality – for instance of an I and a you; a mother and a son; a writer and a reader.

References

Adams, T. E. & Jones, S. H. (2018). The art of autoethnography. In Leavy, P. (Ed.), *Handbook of Arts-Based Research* (pp. 141-64). New York: The Guildford Press.

Atkinson, P. (2006). Rescuing autoethnography. *Journal of Contemporary Ethnography* 35 (4), 400-4.

Ehn, B. & Löfgren, O. (2017). At analysere det oversete. In P.T. Andersen & M. H. Jacobsen, *Kultursociologi og kulturanalyse* (p. 137-65). Copenhagen: Hans Reitzels Forlag.

Ellis, C., Adams, T. E. & Bochner, A. P. (2011). Autoethnography: an overview. *Forum: Qualitative Social Research* 12 (1), 1-18.

Faulkner, S. L. (2018). Poetic inquiry: Poetry as/in/for social research. In P. Leavy (Ed.), *Handbook of Arts-Based Research* (pp. 208-30). New York: The Guildford Press.

Ingold, T. (2007). *Lines: A Brief History*. New York: Routledge.

Ingold, T. (2011). *Being Alive – Essays on Movement, Knowledge and Description*. New York: Routledge.

Ingold, T. (2015). *The Life of Lines*. New York: Routledge.
Leavy, P. (2009). *Method Meets Art*. New York: The Guildford Press.
Leavy, P. (2018). *Handbook of Arts-Based Research*. New York: The Guildford Press.
Manning, Erin (2016). *The Minor Gesture*. Durham: Duke University press.
Mason, J. (2011). Facet Methodology: the case for an inventive research orientation. *Methodological Innovations Online* 6 (3), 75-92.
Mason, J. (2018). *Potent Connections in Personal Life*. Cambridge: Polity Press.
Sloterdijk, P. (2004). *Sphären. Plurale Sphärologie – Band III: Schäume*. Frankfurt am Main: Suhrkamp.
Sloterdijk, P. (2014). *Zur Welt kommen – Zur Sprache kommen* (11th edition). Berlin: Suhrkamp.
Winther, I. W. (2006). *Hjemlighed. Kulturfænomenologiske studier*. Copenhagen: Danmarks Pædagogiske Universitetsforlag.

CHAPTER 3:

The sense and place of sand in day care

Nanna Jordt Jørgensen

Welcome to my sandcastle. It is built on empirical observations of children and adults interacting with sand on playgrounds in Danish day care institutions. These sandy foundations have been decorated with reflections emerging in academic and everyday discussions, and with quotations and theoretical perspectives from favourite texts. Read it before the rain falls, the wind blows, the waves encroach, or the playground attendant comes to sweep it away. You can build it up again, in whatever way you want.

Sand, according to Oxford Dictionaries, is a "loose granular substance, typically pale yellowish brown, resulting from the erosion of siliceous and other rocks and forming a major constituent of beaches, river beds, the seabed, and deserts" (Oxford Dictionaries). Sand surrounds us – as an element of the soil, the ground of the beach, a main component of many building materials, and, if you grow up as a child in Denmark, a key feature of any playground. Furthermore, the 'loose granular substance' described in the dictionary is much more than a dead material created through erosion; sand is also part of socio-material places, sensations, practices and connections.

The motivation behind this chapter is a strong fascination with sand – with the sensous experience of the tiny grains, with the porosity and instability of the material, coupled with its paradoxical heaviness, its massiveness, with its ability to become something else – a castle, a huge concrete building, a glass bowl, a dust cloud – and with its histories rooted in personal and cultural worlds. Doing fieldwork in day care institutions as part of a research project on the encounters between refugee children, their families and Danish day care institutions[1], my attention was drawn to the place of sandpits and sand at playgrounds, and in the everyday life rhythms of – and tensions between – children, social educators[2] and parents. Sand and play in sand are in many ways a porous in-between material and activity, often (although not always) escaping the educational attention of adults, but also featuring a heavy, inescapable and sensuous 'taken-for-grantedness'. The simultaneous insignificance and weighty importance of sand seem to play a part in processes connecting, and sometimes disconnecting, people, materials, places and practices in and beyond day care institutions. This chapter is an attempt to explore these processes through a focus on the relations between sand, sensations and place. The analysis has been intuitively 'made' (Ingold 2013), rather than systematically constructed, resembling, perhaps, a transiently built sandcastle more than an academic text.

Sand – in research and history

My fascination with sand is far from being the first of its kind within the field of social sciences and educational scholarship. Sand underlies and leaks into leisure and work, economy and landscape, sensation and politics, play and learning, and a number of sand studies have paid attention to material, embodied, social and political entanglements of life with sand in different contexts. Ethnographic livelihood studies of sand mining, for instance, have explored how experiences of sand as a potential for personal and communal socio-economic mobility and development entangle with embodied fears of risk and accidents (Hoffmann 2020), the relationships between global trade networks of sand and local livelihood vulnerabilities (Lamb et al. 2019), and the material and political practices and intergenerational conflicts of local sand economies (Jørgensen 2016, 2018). Within tourism studies, explorations of beach sand point to the haptic sensuality of playing with sand when building sandcastles or sunbathing (Obrador-Pons

---

1 See e.g. Bregnbæk, Arent, Martiny-Bruun & Jørgensen, 2017; Jørgensen & Bregnbæk, 2020; Jørgensen & Martiny-Bruun, 2019. The empirical material which I draw on in this chapter consists of fieldnotes and short recordings from fieldwork taking place in a day care institution in a social housing area in 2017.
2 'Social educator' is the official Ministry of Education translation of the Danish term *pædagog*; a member of staff trained in pedagogical theory and practice, including the care of younger children.

2009), and to the complex relationships between sand as material and social imagination (Baldacchino 2010).

In childhood studies, sand and sandpits have been a recurrent theme in discussions about children's play. While earlier discussions centred on the potential for psychological development through sand play (cf. Jarrett et al. 2010), more recent studies explore the entanglements between materiality and imagination in sandpits (Shillington & Murnaghan 2016) and the interrelations between sand and children in play (Taguchi 2011). Historically, sandpits for children's play in urban areas were first developed in Berlin in the second part of the 19th century, and the idea was quickly adopted in other European and North American cities (Jarrett et al. 2010; Shillington & Murnaghan 2016). In Denmark, sandpits were introduced in public playgrounds in Copenhagen in 1908 with the aim of providing clean, safe and healthy spaces for natural activity and creativity for children growing up in urban areas (Coninck-Smith 2017). This specific material organization of children's play was closely related to an intellectual movement which promoted new understandings of childhood and the positive role of play in children's development. Cheap, robust, natural, flexible and open-ended, sand was seen as an ideal element for play and learning through play (Coninck-Smith 1990; Pedersen 2019). In the 20th century, sandpits were prominent features of playgrounds in Europe and North America. While in some places they have disappeared due to fears of health risks (Shillington & Murnaghan 2016), this is not the case in Denmark, where most playgrounds and all day care institutions offer access to a sandpit, and many children spend at least a couple of hours per day playing in or around it.

Sensing sand and making sand cakes

Asma and Mikkel (both 5 years old) are playing together in the large outdoor sandpit at a day care institution situated in a social housing area in a provincial town in eastern Denmark. The toy shovels dig into the sand with a crunchy sound while the children form sand cakes from wet sand and spread fine dry sand over them with their hands.

Mikkel lines up sand cakes on the wooden frame of the sandpit. He tells me about the sand; the heavy, wet sand, which can be formed and used for the construction of cakes, castles and canals; he throws it down, saying: "Look, this is sand, it makes a sound, a rain sound. It is darker." The dry sand, the slippery sand, hot in the sun, which he pours down over the cakes, while grains of sand are dispersed by the wind, is "sugar-sand, it is beach sand, you take it and you pour it." If the sand gets too dry (as in the dry spell of the summer of 2018) you cannot play with it, and the children ask to pour water in the sandpit. Asma seems to like the dry and warm sand, she digs her feet into it, sensing its warm and grainy weight on her skin.

Starting with a photo of a young girl playing with sand in a sandpit, Hillevi Lenz Taguchi (drawing on her work with Karin Hultman), asks: "Is the girl playing with the sand or is the sand playing with the girl?". The author draws on a relational materialist approach, arguing that "the playing is taking place *in-between* the girl and the sand", that sand and child are overlapping and extending forces which resonate in one another (Taguchi 2011, p. 38). Tim Ingold's work on 'making', I suggest, offers us similar insights, but with greater attention to human experience and sentient awareness. A main line of thought in Ingold's work is that the world we inhabit is a meshwork of "entangled lines of life, growth and movement" (Ingold 2011a, p. 63) in which human and more-than-human life interweave. Thus, humans, animals, plants and materials are all participants in the same world, and "the forms that all these creatures take are neither given in advance or imposed from above, but emerge within the context of their mutual involvement in a single, continuous field of relationships" (Ingold 2000, p. 87). This understanding forms the background for Ingold's understanding of 'making'. In processes of making, Ingold argues, people join forces with materials in a "practice of correspondence" (Ingold 2013, p. 108). Correspondence is not a process of interaction in which two disparate parties connect through some kind of bridging operation (Ingold 2013, p. 107). Rather, the parties are open to one another and bind together as lines (cf. Hofverberg 2019). To correspond with the world, Ingold stresses, is "to mix the movements of one's sentient awareness with the flows and currents of animate life" (Ingold 2013, p. 108). Sensuous experience forms part of the correspondences with sand and is a point of entry in my attempts to understand its significance.

Corresponding with sand, as Asma and Mikkel do when making sand cakes, is not just a sensuous, but a multi-sensuous experience, involving, at least, the senses of sight, touch and sound. Clearly, the sense of touch is an important part of the sensation of sand, but as pointed out by Trnka, Dureau & Park, the category of touch encompasses a variety of sensory experiences "including those of hot and cold, pain and pleasure, frizzy and straight, wet and dry, rough and smooth, hard and soft" (Trnka et al. 2013, p. 23). Touching sand means experiencing, for instance, temperature, humidity, and texture. The sensation of sand between fingers tells us not just about the material, but also about its state – wet sand or dry sand, rough sand or fine sand, warm sand or cold sand. Furthermore, sensing sand involves the experiences of touching as well as of being touched – touching sand when playing with it, and being touched by sand as it covers one's feet, or invades shoes and socks, and is blown into hair and eyes.

When Mikkel talks about the different types of sand, he draws our attention to the relations between sensuous experiences of the material and our understandings of its properties. Although the two categories of sand that he distinguishes between could be said to be the same, to Mikkel they are two different kinds because of their different properties. The properties of materials are "neither objectively determined or subjectively imagined, they are practically experienced", and hence processual and relational, Ingold states (2011a, p. 30). Thus, the properties of sand are experienced and sensed in different ways depending on what people *make* with the material, and on which other materials the sand interacts with (e.g. water). To children making sand cakes in a sandpit, the humidity and texture of sand is of key importance. The children experience sand in a different way from the bricklayer mixing sand to make mortar, or young people shoveling and loading sand on lorries while mining sand in dry river beds in Kenya (see e.g. Jørgensen 2016) – they are engaged practically in different activities situated in different places. To Mikkel, the sound and the color of dark sand is a way of describing the sand, but the important property is its constructability. The humidity of the wet, dark sand means that you can build with it. The dry sand, conversely, can be poured; its most important property is its pourability. The properties link to sensations involved in a making process, the making of sand cakes, which is again connected to a particular (kind of) place. Making sand cakes is a practice involving children, sand and some tools, which forms part of everyday institutional life in a day care institution, and which takes place in a sandpit in the playground. However, it is also an activity which is storied in ways that reach beyond the playground.

Making cakes and connections

Asma and Mikkel chat: "I need more sugar," she says. "Then go and get some," he answers. She tells him about the cakes her mother bakes, pancakes, many of them. She pours more sugar. 6-year-old Ann, who is also in the sandpit, tells me: "You can make cakes out of sand. They need water, and the sugar makes it stick. You can make things with sand. We sell the cakes over here. They are very cheap!" A social educator, Sara, is watching the children play. Letting sand pass through her fingers, she tells me that she remembers playing with sand as a child. Her family came to Denmark from Lebanon when she was one year old, and sometimes her father took them to the beach to play.

The process of making sand cakes intertwines with specific sensuous experiences of the material but also with imaginary 'making' activities. Mikkel and Asma do not just make forms from sand through their correspondence with the material; they make cakes, cakes that resemble the cakes their mothers bake. "I make pancakes," Asma tells Mikkel, who answers: "I also bake cakes at home. My mum tries to bake an orange cake." Asma continues: "For my birthday we will have a lot. My mum makes cake. And me. Cakes and pancakes. She helps me." They continue playing, Asma places sand toys around herself, saying, "This is my house. We have nice toys. It is so beautiful. We make pancakes." In this situation, the children do a children's activity in a sandpit, which forms part of the practices going on at this particular place, the playground at the day care institution, but they also make connections to their home. "Something absent – a dream, an image, or a feeling – can attain presence through the materiality of things that we encounter in tactility," Obrador-Pons reminds us in his writings on sandcastles on Menorcan beaches (Obrador-Pons 2009, p. 203). Making sand cakes connects to memories and imaginings of baking real cakes at home as children play with sand and words, and stories arise from and entangle with sensory experiences of sound, taste and touch. Thus, apart from drawing our attention to the different sense experiences involved in touching sand, the children's cake-making also points to the sense of imagination or association usually not included in western categorizations of the senses. Sand becomes sugar and the form which the sand takes from the bucket makes a cake as, in Ingold's words, "the terrains of the imagination and the physical environment [...] run into one another to the extent of being barely distinguishable" (Ingold 2011a, p. 198). Corresponding with sand through touch, the children make forms and stories as they go along: forms, materials, hapticity and play link to memories and imaginations of home life, imaginings which are reengaged in the making process. The making of sand cakes is situated in an actual place and an actual sensuous activity, but the imagining interweaved in the making of sand forms creates connections to other experiences in other places.

As regards the social educator, Sara, the sense of sand also makes connections to other places and other times. While watching the children playing in the sand in the sandpit, she touches the sand, digs her hands into it and lets it run through her fingers, the sensuous experience of the material evoking her own childhood memories of her father taking her to the beach. As Jennifer Mason stresses, sensory memory is not about remembering a single-sense experience, but about the memory of "an *atmosphere* of multiple sensations" (Mason 2018, p. 44). Sara's memories of days on the beach are the memories of the atmospheres of situations and places connected with the material of sand – the sand in the sandpit of the day care institution is not the same as her childhood's sand, but it connects to her memory of playing in sand on a beach as a child.

Casey, building on Merleau-Ponty's thinking on embodied being in place, suggests that places "gather experiences and histories, even language and thought" (1999, p. 24), and that places and bodies 'interanimate' each other (ibid.). Lived and remembered life with sand intertwines with place and creates emotions of belonging. As such, sand makes connections, even as it stays put in its place; in the sandpit. But it does not always stay in place.

Carrying sand, negotiating place and boundaries

Sand in buckets is carried over the playground and mixed with water, mud, soil. Three boys sing a homemade song about mud, hands and clothes smeared in sand and water. Sand is supposed to stay in the sandpit, the adults say. I am sitting on the edge of the sandpit where Ann is playing. "There are different kinds of sandpits," she tells me; "some are made from wood, some have sticks, and some are even made from metal. The ones with bars keep the sand well inside, for a long time. And then there is more water. So it is not sticky."

In his book The Craftsman, Richard Sennett describes how urban planners designing playgrounds in Amsterdam in the post-war period played with ambiguity, for instance by avoiding a clear boundary between grass and sand in the sandpits, hence creating "a live edge, a porous membrane" rather than a strict boundary (Sennett 2008, p. 234). In the design of sandpits in the day care institutions that I have studied in Denmark there is no such deliberate play with ambiguity. Sand is supposed to stay confined in a box (Pedersen, 2019). Certain things may mix, for instance water and sand, but sand and soil are not supposed to mix. The design attempts clear boundaries between sand and non-sand; sand is supposed to be kept in place. However, in practice, sand very often leaks from the sandpit, creating ambiguity in practice although not by design.

"[S]and can easily be out of place," as Shillingtong et al. state (2016, p. 40). The leaking of sand, the boundary transgression, often creates conflictual intergenerational relations. In everyday activities in day care institutions, proper ways and places of playing with sand are constantly negotiated. The children appear quite aware that sand is supposed to be kept in place, as Ann who talks about the well-designed sandpit that keeps sand inside "for a long time". And still, Mikkel digs out big handfuls of sand and places them in his pockets. As he is picked up in the afternoon, his dad sighs, "All that sand. We will have to empty those pockets before you get into the car." In play there are other rules than the ones the adults make; in play, sand spreads over flagstones, grass and soil, moved intentionally by children as well as unintentionally. Children carry sand intentionally: when transgressing the boundaries of 'proper' sand places at the playground as they aim for a good mix of sandy mud; when they carry a sand cake somewhere when playing 'selling cakes'; and when a child aimlessly, it seems, picks up a handful of sand, sensing its texture and brings it along. Pauliina Rautio, in her article about children carrying stones in their pockets, encourages us to appreciate "the momentary and seemingly unguided in children's lives, the fleetingness and aimlessness of autotelic practices" such as picking up stones (Rautio 2013, p. 402), rather than simply focusing on learning outcomes. Spreading sand over grass and flagstones on playgrounds could be seen as such a seemingly irrational practice, which – as a practice without 'measurable significance', in Rautio's words – becomes a political statement (Rautio 2013, p. 405; see also Manning 2016) against the adult ordering of place. However, sand also transgresses boundaries in ways not intended by the children. Bodily boundaries are transgressed, as sand enters eyes, ears, noses and mouths, creates a crunchy, sticky sensation between the teeth, causes tears to run and scalps to itch. And as sand sticks to feet, shoes and clothes and is carried along, with or without the children noticing, sand crosses spatial boundaries and is moved out of the sandpit, spreading over the playground and leaking into buildings.

When sand transgresses boundaries, it produces ambiguous sensations. Mason uses the word 'sensations' to refer to experiences involving multiple senses emerging in relational encounters. Sensations also include extra-sensory experiences, Mason suggests, and emanate from certain environments and situations (Mason 2018, pp. 43, 45). To Danish parents and social educators, the leaking of sand, the sensuous experience of sand out of place, constitutes a small everyday annoyance and discomfort, because sand has to be brought back into the sandpit (if possible), and because sand, sometimes mixed with soil, sticking to clothes or feet, is carried into buildings and here transforms into dirt. But the sensation of sand also appears to link to stronger ambiguous emotions, involving memories of holidays on the beach and the happiness associated with watching children playing in sand, as well as the fear of finding something disgusting in the sandpit – dog droppings perhaps, cigarette butts, condoms, a syringe …? Who uses the sand at night? What is hidden in the heaps? And still, most Danish middle-class parents appear to strongly support the sandpit as a good place for children. Asma's mother appears less convinced.

Sand, discomfort and belonging

Asma is in the sandpit, busily mixing sand with leaves and rowan berries in a bucket. She is making soup. Sara tells me that when her mother and other Syrian parents come to pick up their children and find them playing in the sandpit, they complain. Asma's parents, who recently came to Denmark from Syria, do not like the sandpit. It has an "awful smell", her mum says, remarking that she can smell from a long distance when her daughter has been playing in the sand. Sara says to Asma's mum that the children are playing, and that "sand is quite normal in Denmark. It is part of – everything, actually". Sara's own parents never had a problem with their children playing in sand, she says. But she remembers that her mother gave them a bath every day, it was not up for discussion.

A key debate within anthropological research on senses revolves around the question of whether senses should be approached as 'cultured' – patterned or configured in different ways in different cultures (e.g. Howes 1991) – or with a point of departure in embodied experience (e.g. Ingold 2011b; Pink 2010). Senses are both of these things; as Maurice Merleau-Ponty wrote: "For man, everything is constructed and everything is natural" (Merleau-Ponty 2012, p. 195). The sensation of sand is embodied, situational and linked to sensory memory, but it is also cultured. Godfrey Baldacchino has written about the experience of sand on beaches as one which is "as much mythical as it is tactile and sensory". (Baldacchino 2010, pp. 765-6). In the West, sand signifies time, impermanence, innumerability and recreation, Baldacchino suggests (ibid.). The cultured sensations of sand in Danish sandpits link up with these images, but also, I would suggest, with more regionally or nationally coloured understandings of the national geography, featuring long coastlines, sandy soils, sand dunes, a history of livelihoods based on fishery, as well as of sand drift destroying good agricultural soil. Furthermore, sensations of sand connect to cultural imaginings of childhood and nature, tying beach life to images of autonomous children playing, running freely over white sand dunes or searching for shiny stones on the live edge between waves and sand. Parents with experiences of refugee flight who live with the memories of crossing dangerous waters on their way to Europe[3] may live with other images of sand and therefore sense sand in different ways.

In the introduction to their book, *Senses and Citizenships: Embodying Political Life*, Trnka, Dureau and Park examine the intersections between sensory phenomena and national and supranational forms of belonging, introducing the new concept of sensory citizenship. The making of citizens and citizenship is an ongoing process of inclusions and exclusions, often involving sensory knowledge, they propose (Trnka et al. 2013). I did not get the opportunity to discuss sand with Asma's mother. However, my interviews with other Syrian parents suggest that while they expressed appreciation of the atmosphere of security and trust in Danish day care institutions, a number of everyday practices and materialities left them puzzled. Playing out of doors for several hours during 'school time' and even in cold or wet weather, getting clothes dirty, eating cold, open rye sandwiches for lunch, sleeping outdoors during afternoon naps, and playing in sandpits, or with mud and water, are examples of practices which the Syrian parents emphasized as very different from their educational experiences in Syria, and which they did not immediately recognize as good child rearing practices (Jørgensen, Husted & Madsen 2020; Jørgensen & Bregnbæk 2020). Sara Ahmed, in her book, Queer Phenomenology, proposes

---

3   As part of the research project I interviewed Syrian parents with younger children who all told stories about stressful crossings of the Mediterranean Sea.

that the connections between being in a place and having a place involve the intimacy of coinhabiting spaces with other things (Ahmed 2006, p. 111), which also links with racial and historical dimensions. Ahmed describes migration as a disorientation, hopefully becoming a reorientation, as new places, but also the body, reinhabit new landscapes, smells, sounds and so on (Ahmed 2006, p. 9). The bewilderment about everyday practices and materials in the day care institution described by Syrian parents, and the annoyance with the sandpit exhibited by Asma's mother, for example, may be seen as an element of such disorientation linked to the migration experience.

While most social educators and middle-class parents who grew up in Denmark, like Mikkel's father, may become irritated with the transgression of sand from the sandpit into buildings, cars, hair and skin, this does not seem to destabilize their understanding of sand in sandpits and on beaches as an element of a good childhood. Outdoor play in the sandpit links to notions such as autonomous free play, being outdoors and getting dirty, all highly valued features of childhood in the Scandinavian context (see e.g. Wagner & Einarsdottir 2008). Seen in this light, Sara's account of her parents' support of their children's playing in sand may be considered a statement of embodied belonging to the Danish nationstate (requiring, however, a high level of personal cleanliness). When Sara lets sand run through her fingers while watching the children play, as described earlier, the sensation of sand evokes memories connected to her own life story. But the sensation and Sara's personal memories also intersect with a socio-cultural history of sand and people in the Danish landscape and geography, as well as with the history of the place of immigrants in this landscape, creating a 'hook' (cf. Mogensen, this volume) into Danishness. In this way, Sara's connection to sand may be seen as a potent connection in Mason's terms – arising in intersections between one's own life experience, socio-cultural history and more 'fleeting moments' of association (Mason 2018, p. 190).

What we find in sandfilled cracks and pockets

The short narratives of this chapter are attempts to explore sand and playing in sand as an 'in-between' phenomenon. Sand is a material which appears trivial and taken for granted in the Danish day care context, it seldom attracts focused professional attention, and playing with sand is an activity often taking place in 'cracks' or 'pockets' between other activities. Yet both material and practice carry a potent significance. Following sand in sandpits with attention to sensations and connections to place is a way to approach this significance, yet avoiding pinning it down into fixed boxes.

How do the correspondences between the granular material of sand and children's hands and bodies become significant connections to place(s)? Rather than focusing on the entities that connect, Mason urges us to look at "the connecting", or "the dynamics of the connections themselves". She describes these dynamics as "the betweenness, the emanations and flows, that create a charge, a potency" in the relations involving place, material and people, but also sensations, atmospheres, weather, memory and imagination (Mason 2018, p. 180). The narratives of the chapter suggest that sand is involved in a variety of potent connections evolving in, around and far beyond the day care institution. At the playground, sand and sensations of sand establish and form part of the connections between children, parents, social educators, places and times. Children's multisensory experiences of sand, in processes such as making sand cakes and moving sand, create attachments to the playground as a place, to other children, to home and home experiences, and to adults. To social educators and middle-class parents, sand appears as a natural part of early childhood educational settings. Their sensations of sand give rise to ambiguous emotions, as childhood memories entangle with notions of happy childhoods and the everyday discomfort of sand transgressing boundaries in the present. Newly arrived refugee parents share neither the understanding of the sandpit taken for granted in the day care institution, nor the images attached to the national cultural history; hence, the sensuous experience of sand in sandpits may become a sense of disconnection, of non-belonging to specific places, but also to an education system and a national community. As such, the exploration of sand and sand play also sheds light on the ways in which the experience of coming to a new place is linked to taken-for-granted everyday sensuous experiences of materials in places. 'Nothing much' (Highmore 2011, see chapter 1) happens in the sandpit, yet it offers us insights into the everyday interactions between children, materials and adults in the institutional setting, but also into larger questions about what it means to feel that one belongs, to feel comfortable as a child and a parent in a Danish day care institution. As such, the in-betweenness of relations involving sand at playgrounds is also charged with politics; negotiations about the place of sand, the space for children's agency, and belonging as embodied and emplaced.

I have finished my sandcastle. The wind has started blowing, and we are ready to go back or go on. Would you like to bring a handful of sand with you in your pocket? What does the grainy feeling tell you about places, materials, connections, memories?

References

Ahmed, S. (2006). *Queer Phenomenology: Orientations, Objects, Others*. Durham: Duke University Press.

Baldacchino, G. (2010). Re-placing materiality. *Annals of Tourism Research*, 37(3), 763-78.

Bregnbæk, S., Arent, A., Martiny-Bruun, A. & Jørgensen, N. J. (2017). Statens eller familiens børn? Tvang og omsorg i mødet mellem nytilkomne familier og danske daginstitutioner. *Forskning i Pædagogers Profession Og Uddannelse*, 1 (2), 14.

Coninck-Smith, N. de. (1990). Where Should Children Play? City Planning Seen From Knee-Height: Copenhagen 1870 to 1920. In *Children's Environment Quarterly*, 7 (4), 54-61.

Coninck-Smith, N. de. (2017). Sandkassen som pædagogisk eksperiment i København omkring år 1900. *Dansk Pædagogisk Tidsskrift*, 4.

Hoffmann, M. P. (2020). Digging for sand after the revolution: mafia, labor, and shamanism in a Nepali sand mine. *Dialectical Anthropology*, 1-17.

Hofverberg, H. (2019). *Crafting Sustainable Development. Studies of Teaching and Learning Craft in Environmental and Sustainability Education.* Uppsala University.

Howes, D. (1991). *The Varieties of Sensory Experience: Sourcebook in the Anthropology of the Senses*. Toronto: University of Toronto Press.

Ingold, T. (2000). *The Perception of the Environment: Essays on Livelihood, Dwelling and Skill*. Psychology Press. London and New York: Routledge

Ingold, T. (2011a). *Being Alive: Essays on Movement, Knowledge and Description*. London and New York: Routledge.

Ingold, T. (2011b). Worlds of sense and sensing the world: a response to Sarah Pink and David Howes. *Social Anthropology*, 19 (3), 313-7.

Ingold, T. (2013). *Making: Anthropology, Archaeology, Art and Architecture*. London and New York: Routledge.

Jarrett, O., French-Lee, S., Bulunuz, N. & Bulunuz, M. (2010). Play in the Sandpit. A University and a Child-Care Center Collaborate in Facilitated-Action Research. *American Journal of Play, Fall*, 221-37.

Jørgensen, N. J. (2018). 'Hustling for rights': political engagements with sand in Northern Kenya. In Oinas, E., Onodera, H. & Suurpää, L. (Eds.), *What Politics? Youth and Political Engagement in Africa*. Leiden: Brill.

Jørgensen, N. J. (2016). Schooling, Generation, and Transformations in Livelihoods: Youth in the Sand Economy of Northern Kenya. In Abebe, T., Waters, J. & Skelton, T. (Eds.) *Labouring and Learning* (pp. 1-21). Springer Singapore.

Jørgensen, N. J. & Bregnbæk, S. (2020). *Flygtningebørn i danske daginstitutioner. Pædagogiske dilemmaer og balancegange.* Frederikshavn: Dafolo.

Jørgensen, N. J., Madsen, K. D. & Husted, M. (2020). Sustainability education and social inclusion in Nordic early childhood education. *Zeitschrift Für Internationale Bildungsforschung Und Entwicklungspädagogik – ZEP.* 1. 27-34.

Jørgensen, N. J. & Martiny-Bruun, A. (2019). Painting trees in the wind: socio-material ambiguity and sustainability politics in early childhood education with refugee children in Denmark. *Environmental Education Research*, 1-14.

Lamb, V., Marschke, M. & Rigg, J. (2019). Trading sand, undermining lives: omitted livelihoods in the global trade in sand. *Annals of the American Association of Geographers*, 109 (5), 1511-28.

Manning, E. (2016). *The Minor Gesture*. Durham: Duke University Press.

Mason, J. (2018). *Affinities: Potent Connections in Personal life*. Cambridge; Polity Press.

Merleau-Ponty, M. (2012). *Phenomenology of Perception*. London and New York: Routledge.

Obrador-Pons, P. (2009). Building castles in the sand: Repositioning touch on the beach. *The Senses and Society* 4 (2), 195-210.

Pedersen, L. (2019). Da sandkassen kom til Danmark – sandet der gav legen plads i storbyen. *BUKS – Tidsskrift for Børne- & Ungdomskultur*, 36 (63), 14.

Pink, S. (2010). The future of sensory anthropology/the anthropology of the senses. *Social Anthropology*, 18 (3), 331-3.

Rautio, P. (2013). Children who carry stones in their pockets: on autotelic material practices in everyday life. *Children's Geographies*, 11 (4), 394-408.

Sennett, R. (2008). *The Craftsman*. Bloomsbury: Yale University Press.

Shillington, L. J. & Murnaghan, A. M. F. (2016). Digging outside the sandbox: Ecological Politics of Sand and Urban Children. In Murnaghan, A. M. F. & Shillington, L. J. (Eds.), *Children, Nature, Cities* (pp. 39-56). London & New York: Routledge.

Taguchi, H. L. (2011). Investigating learning, participation and becoming in early childhood practices with a relational materialist approach. *Global Studies of Childhood*, 1 (1), 36-50.

Trnka, S. (2013). *Senses and Citizenships: Embodying Political Life*. London and New York: Routledge.

Trnka, S., Dureau, C. & Park, J. (2013). Introduction. Senses and Citizenship. In *Senses and Citizenship: Embodying Political Life*. London and New York: Routledge.

Wagner, J. T. & Einarsdottir, J. (2008). The good childhood: Nordic ideals and educational practice. *International Journal of Educational Research*, 47 (5), 265-69.

CHAPTER 4:

Attunement to school and classmates

Karen Ida Dannesboe

In the narrow corridor in front of the classroom, a crowd of children has already gathered. It is nearly eight o'clock in the morning and almost the whole of Year 7 is here – sitting, standing or moving around, either in small groups or individually. They chat, laugh and send text messages from their mobile phones. Just arrived, some children struggle to make their way through the crowd, with their school bags on their backs, trying to reach their friends. Some of the girls have shoulder bags, which they squeeze against their bodies with an arm, bag and body becoming one, as they make their way along the narrow passage. Other children have big backpacks hanging from their shoulders, stooping as they walk – apparently weighed down by a heavy school bag. Tightly gathered in groups, many chit-chat, some leaning in so far their shoulders touch. Others sit on the floor, propped up against the wall, seemingly engaged in intimate conversation. They talk about shared interests (films and sport), and about yesterday's events and activities. "Oh no!" one of the girls exclaims, "I forgot to do my homework! Inge [the teacher] will be furious!" Finally, a teacher arrives and unlocks the door to the classroom. Hands grab school bags in varying shapes and sizes and carry them into the classroom. There is the occasional cry of "Where is my bag?", as one of the children flits between classmates in search of the misplaced school bag. Usually, the bag has been deposited against the wall when the children first arrived, but left behind as they rushed to greet their classmates. Upon entering the classroom, children and school bags become scattered. Bodies and bags disconnect. Some bags are thrown onto desks while others hang from the backs of chairs.

Waiting time – a brief moment before the school day formally begins. The field note above, with its description of children's shared conversations and chit-chat, of bodies moving between one another, of school bags and forgotten homework, offers a glimpse into school as part of children's lives. Making my way through the crowds of children in the morning, waiting with them in the corridor, I get an impression of the children's social landscape and the importance of being together. Following the children's social life at school and paying attention to their bodies, behaviour and use of things (school bags, schoolbooks and pencil cases) and to the emergent atmospheres among children, teachers and school environment allows me to explore the micro-processes of being-in-school as a child; i.e., how school comes to matter through children's ways of connecting with each other and with school as a social, material and educational space. In this chapter, I return to empirical material from ten months of fieldwork conducted between 2007 and 2009 among 12-14-year-old schoolchildren in Copenhagen[1], analysing how the children attune to school and classmates in an everyday perspective.

School and children

School is often described as an institutionalised space educating future citizens according to changing civilising ideals and practices (cf. Gilliam & Gulløv 2017). The class is the dominant organising principle in Danish schools (Anderson 2000); there are usually approximately 25-28 children in a class, sharing the same classroom. Most teaching takes place in this classroom, with school lessons often including group work and plenary discussions. The organisation of teaching and lessons is based on ideals of democracy and participation, but also on the idea of the competent child that is capable of making decisions and taking responsibility for its own learning processes. Ethnographic studies of the school emphasise its function as an institutionalised setting that organises children's everyday lives and provides the context for their experiences of education and identity processes (Corsaro 2005; Gilliam 2006; Gilliam & Gulløv 2017; Højlund 2002; James 1993; Thorne 1993; Youdell 2006). Through my fieldwork among schoolchildren, I saw how mundane routines and the organisa-

---

1   The fieldwork included observations of everyday life at school, parent–teacher activities, and visits to the homes of 11 families. In addition, a total of 52 interviews were conducted with 3 teachers, 14 parents and 24 children – with most of the children interviewed at least twice. The empirical data consists of field notes, interview transcripts, and photographs the children took of everyday situations. I have discussed methodological issues and ethical concerns regarding this type of research method elsewhere (see Dannesboe 2012).

tion of time-space affected children in different ways and contributed to their navigations within the physical, social and institutional landscapes of school (Dannesboe 2012). In this chapter, I further pursue this line of thought, but with a particular interest in the brief and often unnoticed moments occurring in-between the formal structures of the school day. These are moments that often escape our attention when studying school as a formative project; moments that might seem insignificant in the formal educative school space, but which matter greatly to the children and their sense-making processes during school hours. In doing so, I focus less on the school as a formative project and institution and more on the children and their movements and doings within the time-space structure in school.

Attunement

The anthropologist Kathleen Stewart argues that studying ordinary life and paying attention to what she calls *pockets* (Stewart 2012) – situations where "things hanging in the air are rhythms worth describing" (Stewart 2011, p. 447) – is an anthropological approach to studying *atmospheric attunement* (ibid.). This chapter sets out to analyse such pockets of atmospheric attunements as they occur in the course of everyday school life. Stewart further describes the relationship between attunement and atmospheres:

> *An atmosphere is not an inert context but a force field in which people find themselves. It is not an effect of other forces but a lived affect – a capacity to affect and to be affected that pushes a present into a composition, an expressivity, the sense of potentiality and event. It is an attunement of the senses, of labors, and imaginaries to potential ways of living in or living through things.* (Stewart 2011, p. 452)

In this way, Stewart claims that affective atmospheres can be understood as a kind of lived affect when being in the world. "Atmospheric attunements are a process of what Heidegger (1962) called worlding – an intimate, compositional process of dwelling in spaces that bears, gestures, gestates, worlds" (Stewart 2011, p. 445). In line with these thoughts, I argue that school life can be understood as a force field of lived affect that children are part of and affected by. This approach helps us to understand the occurrence of shifting intensities in children's daily lives and to grasp minor events that nevertheless come to matter to the children. Stewart focuses on moments as lived affects that catapult the present into composition. I want to further explore the analytical potential of these thoughts in order to comprehend how pockets of atmospheric attunement contribute to children's attunement to school and classmates.

I will argue that attuning oneself to school and classmates is not only a matter of knowing the school's formal structures and rules, but of being attuned through sensations and through a sense of connectedness with each other and with the practices of school. In her work on affinities, the British sociologist Jennifer Mason (2018) describes affinities "as potent connections that rise up and matter" (Mason 2018, p. 1). She argues that we can explore "affinities that can arise as sparks and charges in animated places, things, technologies, journeys and across all of these, in socio-atmospherics of living" (Mason 2018, p. 168). By paying attention to the socio-atmospherics of living and the connectedness between people, things, places and, in a broader sense, the environment, we can grasp the character, potency and significance of affinities. The aim is not to point out connections between people, things and places, but to address the quality of affinities as they come into being in sensory and bodily experiences of being in the world. Studying children's bodily and social interactions brings us closer to an understanding of the ways in which affinities and close relationships are created in children's everyday lives (Davies 2012). In line with this approach, I study affinities occurring in-between children and their everyday school environment by empirically exploring children-being-in-school as sensory-bodily experiences and connections charged by the flow of energy between children's bodies, ordinary school artefacts and the school as an institutionalised time-space structure.

Mason does not refer directly to Stewart's concept of atmospheric attunement, but in a broader sense, she alludes to a kindred set of ideas represented in Stewart's earlier work on ordinary affects (2007). I am particularly interested in the way that sparks and charges and emerging affinities come to matter in atmospheric attunements. With this analytical twist, I explore how children's attunement to school, classmates and the abundance of artefacts present in this socio-spatial environment are constituted through, and also reach beyond, the above-mentioned pockets of atmospheric attunements. Following Stewart's idea of studying pockets, I analyse what can be understood as three different pockets, all of which might present themselves as seemingly minor events at first glance, but that emerge and are repeated within ordinary school life as small cracks in teacher-initiated activities and the time-space structure of school.

Cracks in the educative space of school – a place for friendships

It is quiet in the classroom. We are in the middle of a lesson; the students are working on an assignment. Each child at a desk. The teacher assists students who ask for help. Once in a while, there is the sound of whispering voices, a creak as students move around in their chairs. The sound of pencils on paper also reaches my ears. A pencil drops to the floor. Meanwhile, Lea moves her body from her desk across the room to Laura's desk. She moves quietly, carrying a pencil in her hand. Whispering, she asks Laura if she can borrow her pencil sharpener. While using the pencil sharpener, she squats next to Laura's desk where they whisper together, creating a moment for hushed private conversation within the otherwise teacher-structured time and space. During the lesson, other gestures and acts take place; children's bodies slowly and silently move around with the excuse of borrowing things from each other, going to the bathroom or getting help from one another without causing too much of a disturbance and while evading the teacher's attention. Natasja moves from her place at the back of the classroom. She glances at the teacher, who is busy helping another student. Without making much noise, she quickly crosses the room and, with a sliding movement, finds herself a chair next to Freja. While the teacher talks about the next assignment, they lean across the desk, drawing on each other's pencil cases and writing each other's names on their school bags, giggling and chitchatting in whispered voices. Their bodies are close together; their arms and shoulders touch each other as almost one-body-with-pencils. Every now and then, they lift their heads, glance at the teacher and return to drawing. They are engaged in each other and their shared activity while still paying (some) attention to the teacher.

During my fieldwork, individual or group work with specific assignments was a common part of a normal school day. The school day was structured in 45-90-minute lessons, with breaks in between, and spatially organised in classrooms, corridors and outdoor areas. In the classroom, children's bodies were placed at desks and chairs according to the teachers' decisions regarding who should be seated where and next to whom in order to reduce noise and maintain order in the classroom (see e.g. Dannesboe 2012). My observations show that students were very much aware of the institutional norms for appropriate behaviour. They knew that too loud voices and animated bodies would be sanctioned by the teachers. However, within this organisation of children's bodies, orchestrated by the teachers for teaching purposes, cracks were made in order to create or maintain social relations. As the passage above shows, this often came about by positioning one's body next to a classmate, by silently moving from one chair to another in an attempt to get close to one another, or with an excuse to move around (the need to borrow a pencil or an eraser).

Stewart describes attunement as a way to link or connect to the world's texture, where "the body has to learn to play itself like a musical instrument in this world's compositions" (2010, p. 450). Applying this metaphor, children act as instruments in the composition of the school. Attuning themselves to the teacher's instructions and using their knowledge of school norms and what teachers view as appropriate behaviour, the children smoothly bend the strict composition of school. The behaviours described above can be seen as small improvisations within the orchestration of school lessons – actions that create small variations of the well-known 'school melody' but remain in key with the general organisation of school lessons. These improvisations provided parallel or small in-between spaces in the formalised educative space afforded by the school. Sharing each other's school supplies seems to be a way of maintaining and reaffirming relations between classmates and friends, and in doing so, practising a sociality that remains within the parameters of what is recognised as acceptable behaviour at school. Tim Ingold (2015) argues that clinging to people and things is one way through which humans become part of the world and through which we maintain our existential footing. The intensified minor events involving bodily gestures and borrowing practices become a way to cling to each other and the school as a social world. The embodied practices and the physical proximity create temporary animated social spaces within ordinary school routines. Such practices enable social connectedness with friends and classmates.

On the edge – football and making school a meaningful place

The bell rings. The break is over. Many of the children are already in the classroom finding their seats. The teacher enters the classroom, closes the door and asks them to be quiet. The sound of children's voices fades, chairs scrape against the floor as the children sit down. One minute later, the door suddenly opens and a group of boys stumble into the room. They talk to each other in loud voices, have rosy cheeks and their bodies are charged with energy expressed in their swift movements and gestures. One of them is carrying a football. They are discussing some of the hard tackles made in their football match and who won. They have run to class from the field having just finished the match. The teacher hushes them: "Keep quiet! You are late! Why can't you be on time?" The boys' voices fade as their bodies disentangle and they hurry to their seats. After a while, their bodies have calmed down; some of them are facing the teacher while others stare out of the window. Perhaps still thinking about football.

During my fieldwork, a group of 5-7 boys frequently entered the classroom a few minutes after the lesson had begun. Energy-charged bodies, rapid movements and vivid conversations filled the previously calm classroom with an animated atmosphere. Usually, one of the boys was carrying a football. During our informal conversations, the boys told me that football was the best thing about school. Observing them and their daily interactions, football was clearly a central aspect of their school life. They played football almost every day during the breaks between lessons. The moment the bell rang, they took off with the football, heading for the field on the other side of the school grounds. For some of them, but not all, football also played a central role in their lives outside school, but during school hours it became a shared activity and a way of being together.

Most of the boys in this group did not find school life easy. They explained that they did not always understand what they were supposed to do, and described how they struggled with the assignments given by teachers. As a result, they often paid little attention to what was going on during lessons. Observing their behaviour during lessons, I noticed that they often did not participate much in classroom activities. As described above, they were often scolded for arriving late for lessons, for being too noisy during lessons or for being unprepared and not paying attention to what the teachers said.

It seems as lessons drain their bodies of energy, while playing football is an energising event, making them lively, active and engaged in a shared activity. This transformation from the animated collective-body-with-ball to somewhat inattentive and non-participating boys appears to be an embodied and experienced attunement to school. As Lisa Proctor has shown in her ethnographic study of schoolchildren, children's embodied experiences at school are part of meaning-making and relationship-building processes (Proctor, 2015). As Proctor states with reference to Stewart (Stewart 2007), "affective repertoires and choreographies of everyday life encompass states of both resonance, as they connect with past events, and potentiality, as they direct and shape unfolding future events" (Proctor 2015, p. 132). The boys' attunement to school resonates with contrasting school experiences, as described above. From the teachers' perspective, it might seem as though these boys are teetering on the edge of school, paying little attention to formal educative school space. However, their animated collective-body-with-ball can also be seen as part of their collective embodied attunement to school – as a way of dealing with the rigid school structure, the academic demands and lessons that they considered boring. Arriving late for lessons and filling the school space with an animated atmosphere creates a crack in the structure of school – a crack in which the boys' collective practice and energised bodies charge the school space with a form of vivid social energy, creating affinities to one another and to the school despite the alienating experiences that characterise other aspects of their school lives. Football fuels shared practices and the creation of an in-between space and social community, but it also serves as a kind of connection enabling the boys to maintain a relation to school. For this group of boys, their shared practice is a potential source of school engagement, with football, rather than lessons, being the key to their sense of belonging at school. In this sense, teetering-on-the-edge is a particular attunement to school, in which children transform alienating experiences into meaningful shared practices within the boundaries of school.

Awkwardness – feeling out of place

> *Biology. The teacher is standing in front of the blackboard talking about the topic of today's lesson, focused on a passage in the textbook. He asks the students to take the book out of their bags and to form groups for reading and discussing the text. Several of the children have left the book at home; some start reading. Lisa is sprawled comfortably in her seat, rocking the chair back and forth while her school bag lies on the table. It is closed. The teacher approaches her and asks her to take out her book. She claims that she did not bring it with her today. The teacher becomes more insistent: standing close to her on the other side of the table, he asks her again in a firm voice. Slowly, she pulls a few books from her bag, looks up at the teacher and repeats that she did not bring the book. The teacher follows her movements and examines the books now laid out on the table, but he does not look in the bag. There seems*

to be an invisible boundary marking the school bag as the children's private space. Annoyed, he asks her to join a group of children and read with them.

This kind of non-participation was often expressed by children's postures, such as putting their feet up on the table, crossing their arms and turning their body towards the windows or other children instead of the teacher, throwing pieces of paper or other small objects across the room – actions that the teachers saw as disruptive. As the above passage with Lisa illustrates, children use their bodies and things (school bags, paper etc.) to challenge teachers' authority to define the classroom situation. As other studies have shown, such behaviour can be interpreted as opposition to institutional norms (see e.g. Gilliam 2010; Gulløv 2009; McDermott 1996). However, observing the children throughout the school day and listening to their experiences, such oppositional situations also comprise what Stewart calls affective atmospheres: a tension, awkwardness and discomfort manifested in bodies, gazes and voices. In the example with Lisa, in the brief moment where the teacher is waiting for her to reach for her books, the material, bodily and social connections co-create an atmosphere charged with tension and an undefinable energy. This connection between the teacher, Lisa and the books can be understood as a kind of lived affect of discomfort and mistrust. This discomfort and mistrust are further animated by Lisa and other children's experiences with their teachers – experiences of teachers criticising them for being unprepared and for not trying hard enough. For instance, Lisa explained that she did not ask for help anymore (even though she struggled with many school assignments) because the teachers got angry with her when she did not understand their explanations. She said that "sometimes it is better not to understand at all", because then she could escape the teachers' reactions. These experiences, and the discomfort they caused, led Lisa to say that she hated school.

In this sense, the moments charged with discomfort and mistrust resonate with the children's prior experiences and affect them and their general attunement to school. As Mason argues, affinities are a kind of potent connection experienced viscerally and personally. They are sparks and charges of connections that are lived locally and come to life through embodied experiences (Mason 2018). In the case of Lisa, ineffable charges and atmospheres of tension arose in situations where the contact between Lisa and her teachers involved confrontation, discussion and disagreement – atmospheres of tension that resonate with her recurrent experiences of being out of place at school and feelings of awkwardness, mistrust and self-doubt. Embodied experiences evoke a fragile relation to school for children such as Lisa. Such fragile relations comprise an attunement to school, co-created by children, teachers and artefacts like school bags and schoolbooks, that pushes students like Lisa away from school as a meaningful social and educational space and turns it into a space of discomfort and alienation.

Conclusion

In this chapter, I have explored potent connections between children, between children and things, and between children and teachers through what Stewart refers to as 'pockets' – brief moments in children's everyday lives where they connect to each other and to school as a lived, experienced and institutionalised space. The focus on pockets and minor events highlights the affective and dynamic aspects of ordinary life that emerge in brief moments in time and space – not detached from the school as an institution, but entangled within it. The moments explored in this chapter are metaphorical cracks occurring within the ordinary time-space structure of school and teacher-defined/orchestrated educational activities. As the analysis illustrates, school is much more than a formal learning space; it is a social world where affinities arise in-between human and more-than-human participants, where small cracks in the formal school structure pave ways for counter-activities and practices that support different forms of clinging to school, or where seemingly disruptive forms of behaviour enable unforeseen forms of participation. It is through the existence of such affinities that school becomes a meaningful social world. The three pocket phenomena analysed in this chapter involve different entanglements of children's bodies, school-related artefacts and formal school structures in moments charged with affects that resonate with past experiences of school and ongoing social practices. Artefacts can fuel such processes, enabling sparks and charges in children's social lives, creating potent connections in children's different ways of attuning themselves to school and their classmates. The school as a social world becomes familiar over time, but, for some children, it also contains alienating elements as being-in-school resonates with experiences of being wrong and feeling out of place. Analysing the brief moments within or at the edge of the formal school structure and studying children's mutual bodily and social engagements as part of their school day allows us to see beyond the official formative project of schooling. Social processes take place both in-between and as integral parts of everyday school routines and the formative project of educating children. These social processes are mediated by the school space and by artefacts that connect children to each other and to school environments in ways other than those prescribed by formal schooling. In this sense, such analysis of cracks, embodied sensations and lived affects reveals other sides of contemporary schooling as it takes place and is given meaning by children.

References

Anderson, S. (2000). *I en klasse for sig*. Copenhagen: Gyldendal Uddannelse.

Corsaro, W. A. (2005). *The Sociology of Childhood*. Thousand Oaks, London, Delhi: Pine Forge Press.

Dannesboe, K. I. (2012). *Passende engagement og (u)bekvemme skoleliv. Et studie af børns navigationer mellem skole og familie*. (PhD thesis). Aarhus University,

Davies, H. M. (2012). Affinities, seeing and feeling like family: Exploring why children value face-to-face contact. *Childhood, 19*(1), 8-23.

Gilliam, L. (2006). *De umulige børn og det ordentlige menneske. Et studie af identitet, ballade og muslimske fællesskaber blandst etniske minoritetsbørn i en dansk folkeskole*. (Ph.d. afhandling). Danmarks Pædagogiske Universitet, Copenhagen.

Gilliam, L. (2010). Den gode vilje og de vilde børn: Civiliseringens paradoks i den danske skole. *Tidsskriftet Antropologi, 62*, 153-74.

Gilliam, L., & Gulløv, E. (2017). *Children of the Welfare State: Civilising Practices in Schools, Childcare and Families*. London: Pluto Press.

Gulløv, E. (2009). Barndommens civilisering. Om omgangsformer i institutioner. In S. Højlund (Ed.), *Barndommens organisering* (pp. 115-47). Frederiksberg: Roskilde Universitetsforlag.

Højlund, S. (2002). *Barndomskonstruktioner: på feltarbejde i skole, SFO og på sygehus*. Copenhagen: Gyldendal Uddannelse.

Ingold, T. (2015). *The Life of Lines*. New York: Routledge.

James, A. (1993). *Childhood Identities: Self and Social Relationships in the Experience of the Child*. Edinburgh: Edinburgh University Press.

Mason, J. (2018). *Affinities. Potent Connections in Personal Life*. Cambridge: Polity.

McDermott, R. P. (1996). The acquisition of a child by learning disability. In S. Chaiklin & J. Lave (Eds.), *Understanding Practice. Perspectives on Activity and Context* (pp. 269-305). Cambridge: Cambridge University Press.

Proctor, L. (2015). 'No, You've Done it Once!': Children's expression of emotion and their school-based place-making practices. In A. Hackett, L. Proctor, & J.

Seymour (Eds.), *Children's Spatialities. Embodiment, Emotion and Agency* (pp. 128-45). Houndmills, Basingstoke, Hampshire: Palgrave Macmillan.

Stewart, K. (2007). *Ordinary Affects*. Durham & London: Durham University Press.

Stewart, K. (2011). Atmospheric Attunements. *Environment and Planning D: Society and Space, 29.* doi:10.1068/d9109.

Stewart, K. (2012) Pockets. *Communication and Critical/Cultural Studies*, 9:4, 365-8, DOI: 10.1080/14791420.2012.736161

Thorne, B. (1993). *Gender Play. Girls and Boys in School.* Buckingham: Open University Press.

Youdell, D. (2006). *Impossible Bodies, Impossible Selves: Exclusions and Student Subjectivities.* Dordrecht: Springer.

CHAPTER 5:

The companion city – an initial ramble

Jon Dag Rasmussen

Street corner and contact venue in Copenhagen.

Morning. Wakening.
Invited by the rays of the sun. Initiated by the rays of the sun. The street corner is wrapped in one of its many daily disguises as elderly men return from the kiosk to rest their legs on the deep blue container. One by one they are drawn into the city, entering the streets from their living arrangements: the small apartments and rooms scattered throughout the city sphere. Smokes are lit with shaking hands. Snapping and short exchanges. Small comments and greetings. A strange atmosphere looms in the air between brick walls, pieces of concrete sidewalk, surfaces and facades. Hostility? Despair? Expressions of loneliness? An urgent need to escape the confinement of solitude and restricted space? Green milk crates enter the hesitant, subtle and almost silent exchange, when more seats are needed. They linger on the sidewalk as witnesses of the assembly, and as monuments that reach further on into the day.
Wakening. Morning.

Introduction

In the arts and in works of poetry it is often explored how cities or landscapes take on the appearance, character and feeling of personified companions (see e.g. Hede & Kjølner Hansen 2014; Laugesen 2016; Strindberg 2016; Ørntoft 2014). Furthermore, the idea that walks, ventures and stops in various landscapes and environments call forth a curious and tightly woven coherence between human and other-than-human elements is also found in Western-based academia (see Dunn 2016; Lund 2012; Petersen 2017; Taussig 2015) as well as in numerous cross-border academic writings (e.g. Solnit 2001; Thoreau 2014). This points towards the phenomenon that human beings in their movement and involvement can attain a synthesis, or an experience of coherence with the world – a blurring of conventionally accepted[1] boundaries between the corporality of the human and the corporality of the world (e.g. Ingold 2007). This conception is not new to ethnography and anthropology as different scholars engaged in non-Western contexts have been working with such *ecologies* for decades (e.g. Feld 1982; Kohn 2013; Willerslev 2007). Meanwhile, in contemporary big-city research within fields such as sociology, human geography, urban studies and urban anthropology, this dimension is rarely part of the presented and written analytical work.

In this chapter, I draw on empirical knowledge acquired during long-term ethnographic fieldwork conducted in Copenhagen between 2011 and 2016[2]. The fieldwork was carried out among research participants I have come to describe as 'unusual elderly people'[3] – people that possess ordinary, or close-to-ordinary, housing facilities but spend most of their waking hours on spidery, entangled and surprisingly strange paths of movement and small-scale mobility – practices taking them through the cityscape (e.g. Rasmussen 2017b). My primary aim in this piece is to show how the city works as an other-than-human companion in the lives of select unusual elderly people. The chapter approaches and unfolds how an empirically pronounced and

---

1 In Western societies and contexts at least.
2 The research project was co-financed by Aalborg University, Department of Sociology and Social Work and the EGV Foundation (Social inclusion of older adults).
3 The rather vague and imprecise concept of 'unusual' (cf. the Danish term *usædvanlige* that could also translate as e.g. *unconventional*) is chosen to avoid the many ethnographically inappropriate meanings, (scientific and normative) prejudices and correlations found in more well-established conceptions of *marginalised, deviant* and the like.

broadly resonating experience with *the city as a companion in everyday life* is prevalent among the participants, albeit that it remains a verbally understated and inarticulate phenomenon. In this regard, the companion qualities explored here constitute both a shared experience and an individual encounter with the city organism that materialise during the application and appropriation of accessible public and pseudo-public space. The companion city is an omnipresent creature affording significant cracks and rifts in which to live, delve, rest and dwell for some people. The cityscape is teeming with interstices and in-between possibilities that appear and apply to particular citizens.

A major prerequisite for apprehending the contribution is that the people followed in the ethnographic involvement all possess living arangements as a consequence of the Danish Welfare Model. This system ensures that fundamental needs such as social benefits, basic health care and living arrangements are covered as soon as people consent to this support. Due to this circumstance the research participants described all possess a roof over their heads, whether it be individual apartments, studio-type rooms or rooms in special-unit nursery homes dedicated for active substance users.

Furthermore, in terms of form, the chapter is executed in a practice (of writing, thinking, presenting) I have previously tried to frame with the concept of an *alchemical research style* (Rasmussen 2016, unpublished). This implies that different elements are brought together in the attempt to test their reciprocal and generative powers. Being an alchemical researcher is characterised by a will to bring very different, at times conflicting, elements into the academic workshop, to mix substances in the search of hitherto unnoiticed or unacknowledged analytical potentials, and to experiment with textual and descriptional thickness and thinness as well as unexplained textual and/or intellectual gaps, subtle parallels and open-ended arguments. When uneven elements such as lyrics, philosophy, social research, literature and experimental writing are mixed with empirical-based acknowledgements, it is part of this endeavour at redeeming things otherwise mute or dim[4] through attempts at doing research in alchemical ways. Integral to this form is the need for explicit and active participation of the reader since intellectual and analytical involvement is anticipated as well as necessary to complete the work. Throughout the chapter

---

4 See Theodor Adorno 2005, p. 247 for the inspiration for this particular wording.

my aim is to draw different parts, elements and knowledges[5] together, to hit notes, chords, lines of melody, to play with references and re-affirmations that provide potential and gather atmospheres and feelings across different sources, to collect and combine perspectives all able to reflect and contribute to a notion of *the companion city*, to assemble stuff around this conceptual thinking-pillar, to compose, to ramble along, to contemplate, to speculate, to write music(ally).

Blurry encounters – taking flight from the street corner

The street bench is a set of assistant bones. A scaffolding affording itself to the choirs of moving matter inherent to the cityscape. Folded into this framework of iron and wood for hours on end, distances between (the) elderly man and (his) surroundings decrease. A blur.[6]
    Watching becomes daydreaming.
        Daydreaming becomes absorption.
            Absorption becomes fusion-like, a fusion-like presence.

"Bird" spent his days and evenings in the public realms of the city. I knew[7] him as a consequence of this public presence that took place in the vicinity of his third-storey apartment. In the warm months he stayed outside, following the rays of the sun as they hit street benches and curbs on which he resided, an elderly and utterly skinny man. Most often he was alone, almost always alone, a lone man, a painter of lone()lines(s) in the cityscape. He lived his everyday life in a radius of approximately 250 meters around his formal housing arrangement; the small apartment. His walk was poor, slow, troublesome. Still, he fought his way to the benches, until he day he dropped. These benches, as well as other

---

5 The plural form of this term refers to Donna Haraway's work on *situated knowledges* that emphasise how all knowledge is positional (1988). In this context it is also used to underscore how traditions such as art, research and philosophy tend to approach phenomena through different perspectives and vocabularies.

6 A phrase borrowed from Danish artist MØ, "… let me out, I'm trapped in a blur …" (MØ (2018), *Blur,* track 3: Forever Neverland).

7 In this sentence, the past tense employed refers to both the time of the actual fieldwork and to Bird's life that found its end in 2015.

distinct and indistinct parts of the city are informal institutions that helped him carry his existence.

This pattern of *roaming the city*, although variable in terms of distance, preferences and the proximity to fellow beings, is prominent among the large body of elderly people I came to know through fieldwork. They stay, wander and move about in the public sphere, in the company of human and non-human acquaintances, and in the company of an ever-present city-being.

I have followed along as these urban dwellers leave their claustrophobic, often distressing, threatening and small apartments to indulge in a much broader *being with the city.* On the streets they engage in low-frequency exchanges, a contact of a both immediate and yet withdrawn and vague kind. They wander from daylight into the dark. For some of these people, many kilometres are traveled on foot; for others their wanderings are limited in physical scope, but deep in terms of experience, significance and weight. In all cases their trails lead into a city that is encountered and entered by extensive and persistent presence. Metaphorical trapdoors are breached and the city opens up its nooks and crannies to such tenacious and seeking inhabitants – the city is a house; its streets, bridges, strips, tunnels and arcades are also rooms, hallways, attics, balconies, chambers, basements, stairwells.[8]

To commute and to move about is also to communicate in a sense, to change[9] and to enter into crucial processes of exchange in and with the city. It goes for most of us, the urban human dwellers, that we leave our apartments during the day to mingle with others in the vastness of the city. That we take off in the morning to return in the afternoon or into the evening. The special case with the people followed in this work is that they flee existing formal housing to merge into the urban world on profound although indistinct levels. Park sites, public benches, secondhand stores, intersections, street corners, curbs etc. constitute the specific and concrete goals for their everyday ventures. But the companion they seek and eventually reach, the creature they accompany, accommodate, immerse into, temporarily dissolve with and follow along, is the

---

8   See Bachelard (1994) on the phenomenological aspects of inhabiting houses. See also Rasmussen, 2020, p. 96, 233.

9   Cf. the etymological heritage of the term *commute* "to change (something into something else), to transform" from Latin *commutare* "to often change, to change altogether", from *com-* + *mutare* "to change, go, move" (see https://www.etymonline.com/search?q=commute, accessed on February 23rd, 2021).

being that British urbanist Nick Dunn has described as a *superorganism* (Dunn 2016, p. 37) – the city.

The work on which this chapter draws has shown how movement and the extensive presence in the city sphere among the elderly leads towards different kinds of absorption. The city is often described as a loud complex of numerous distractions, a machine that produces manifold forms of alienation and distances in daily life, a brute force that colonises and enters the human body to evoke certain effects (e.g. Simmel 1950). Meanwhile, in the case of the elderly people followed it also constitutes a diffuse kind of company – a sometimes accessible and present companion of substantial importance to everyday life.

> fold the map, **mend the gap**
> **and I tow the word companion**
> and I make my **self escape**
> oh, the **multitude of other**
> Bon Iver, "29 #Strafford APTS".

The ability and need to **escape**[10], to fuse into the loop of a metropolitan sphere always teeming with **other**s; beings, artifacts, fumes, atmospheres, dust. This subtle kind of dissolution – a need to absorb into (an)**other** – is found among the elderly as they frequent particular street corners, sidewalks, storefronts, **gap**s between buildings, pieces of asphalt and concrete, back rooms and the calm fringes of charitable organisations. The jagging of the classical and uniform *psychological* **self** is no new invention in either the social sciences[11], the biological sciences[12], or elsewhere; neither is a blurring of the conventional separation between e.g. humans and a **multitude of other** organisms, beings and critters.[13]

Along the lines of movement and stops reaching through the urban landscape, ordinary distinctions between **self** and **other**, elderly people and the broader

---

10 In the following sections I employ the poetics of the cited lyrics (marked in **bold**) in my writing. This approach is an experiment towards an explicit use of poetic and lyrical imagery in the making of scientific analysis.
11 E.g. Blumer 1986; Asplund 1987.
12 Gilbert 2017.
13 E.g. Haraway 2008, 2016; Costandi 2012; Rees et. al 2018.

environment, are blurring. Drawing on Katrín Lund's work, it is possible to understand this phenomenon in terms of 'a merge' – a dissolution of normatively constructed and taken-for-granted boundaries (Lund 2012). The concrete tiles and cobblestones of the sidewalk fuse with the walking human (ibid.), the ever-present fumes, particles and atmospheres cross boundaries between urban, human and other-than-human systems. This *blurring* **mend**s **the gap**s and crevices we usually expect and (subsequently) find in the world around us, (intellectual) gaps installed to separate humans from non-human stuff.[14]

When experiencing the world alongside the elderly research participants, narrowly defined notions of **self** periodically cease to exist as they momentarily, for short glimmers and for longer interludes, seem to **escape** the confinement of selfhood during meetings and merges with a **multitude of other** urban inhabitants and beings. To *stretch everyday life into the city*[15] is to give oneself up to movement, to cease existing as a bounded (id)entity, to undergo change, to process and to handle harsh everyday life conditions by throwing one's existence into the surging currents of the city. **I tow the word companion** (cf. the excerpt above) is towing and throwing one's body out into the open to accompany and merge periodically with a teeming superorganism. It is 'letting go' by allowing disturbances, sound, light, rain, wind, elements, matter, organisms and lifeforms to enter, perforate, disorganise and disturb the constitution of the so-called human self. To stretch everyday life into the city is to feed on others and otherness by sacrificing identity and singularity in a narrow sense of such notions. Based on ethnographic accounts, conversations and countless days shared on street corners, park areas, in secondhand stores, bars and in movement through vast distances of the asphalt world, what seems to be the case is that another openness – a blurry state of being in and with the city – becomes reachable in the realm of the urban landscape.

---

14 A product and a remnant of Western Enlightenment philosophy, see e.g. Haraway 2016; Morton 2016, 2017.
15 A conceptual imagery developed to describe this particular kind of street life (Rasmussen 2017a).

On the acquisition of company, peace and more-than-individuality

Pigeons and crows are
>roaming and awaiting in the churchyard. As he approaches, they gather and
>>welcome him with greetings, with attentive gestures,
>
>with flickering eyes. Grains and seeds distributed on the ground, picked up, eaten. Companion beings at work. Existences to follow, to live along. Partakers of/in the city. As if holding hands, as handles, as if holding on – imperceptible strings catching
>>>onto each other. Into each other.
>>>Stringing (each-/an-) other.[16]

My contention is that the city allows for some elderly people to enter a more-than-individual state of being. In the pseudo-poetic paragraph above it is described how a man encounters and merges with this extensive organism comprising various elements that flow through and are alive in the cityscape. The residency and movement practised by the people followed support the achievement of a salutary, although limited, peace. Peace from experienced everyday confinements, peace from undesirable thinking patterns and haunting ideas of self-referential and self-centered kind, peace from a noisy self (see Rasmussen 2017a). In visiting benches and park sites, when frequenting particular street corners and other places in the urban realm, and when walking through well-known territory, parts and quarters of the city, such feelings are resolved, at least partially, temporarily. The main components in this process are the acts of walking, movement and outside residency, the experience of sights, other sensory influences and the meetings with the myriad 'stuff' of the city that arises here. The diversions, distractions and pursuits inherent to this kind of presence and participation holds a key to understanding how movement evokes feelings of freedom, peace and affinity with others and otherness. It paves the way, too, to acknowledging how the stimuli encountered *en route* enable more-than-individual and de-individualising possibilities and potentials. This analysis resonates with a number of perspectives found in research as well as in non-academic literature. In Robert Desjarlais' ethnography *Shelter Blues* (1997) the

---

16 Cf. Donna Haraway's work on various types of "strings" and "string figures" (2016).

reader is drawn into the world of inhabitants in a Boston shelter for homeless people, of whom many also live with extensive substance use and mental problems. Desjarlais describes how movement plays a crucial role among some of the residents as it seems to resolve and mend tensions and complications in their everyday situations. Similar needs and patterns arise among the elderly people on the streets of Copenhagen. In the excerpt below, Desjarlais notes how some informants enter and pace through the city in pursuit of a certain state of mind:

> *Too much calm could get to a person after a while, however, and many tried to find ways to keep busy without getting bored. An idle mind was an ill mind for some; pacing and other routines helped to lessen the worries that came with living in the shelter.* (1997, p. 19)

Whereas it is well established in social scientific contexts that routines can work as complexity-reducing security webs and installations in many people's lives (e.g. Ehn & Löfgren 2010), spatial practices, so-called 'pacing' and the experiences and sensory stimuli encountered in movement can be supportive to this end as well. The same notion is found in Paul Auster's neo-classical novel *The New York Trilogy* (Auster 2008) where the protagonist, a man named Quinn, gradually slips into the city "by giving himself up to the movement of the streets, by reducing himself to a seeing eye" (ibid., p. 10-11), a spectator and a meticulous observer of the everyday, whereby he escapes the obligation to think – an **escape** that provides a measure of peace in the life of a restless and gradually dissolving man.

By scrutinising specific street corners and other public and pseudo-public places in Copenhagen, it is possible to understand such very ordinary and mundane installations as *venues of contact* between unusual elderly people and the broader city-organism. These places appear as portal-like cracks and 'pockets' to some, while being ordinary components and elements of the city to others. As the small opening text of this section shows, a distinct part of a churchyard can comprise such a crack or venue. Pigeons and crows are birds and creatures in their own right, in the same way as the elderly man, the grains, the seeds and the churchyard site are entities with their own physical borders. But at the same time, they are all partakers in the situation described, as they gather, initiate and engage in different forms of contact, and accompany each other for a while. The situation is a result of movement in various forms, and of lines of life (cf. Ingold 2015) all drawn to the same place where they entangle, encircle and enmesh. The participants in this situation are all singular entities as well as an entanglement of interests and lives cast in a whirlwind. In the terminology of Jennifer Mason (2018), these interests and seemingly simple relational entanglements comprising different beings (and 'beings' in a very broad definition also including conventionally inert stuff) initiate sparks and catalyse energies and atmospheres of affinity in the presence of each other. In much the same way as when heat and ultimately fire develop from the entanglement of wooden sticks, human stubbornness and movement; when encounter-becomes-movement-becomes-sparks-becomes-fire, these meetings in and with the city also generate relational sparks and energy and lead to affinities, experienced intensities and fire. Following the man described above over an extended period of time has shown how he accompanies the wild birds in very literal ways, that the exact spot in the churchyard is where the motley congregation meet, and that the company happening here plays a significant role in his everyday life. When dissecting this situation analytically, the primary participants count as follows: a man, a number of wild birds, fodder, a particular part of a churchyard facility. Movement, interests and needs are what enable the encounter and binds the gathering together for a while on a given day, and recurrently over time. It is also possible to understand the situation as an integral part of larger-scale urban life given that the churchyard is part of contexts such as the city quarter and ultimately the city as a whole. This approach makes it possible to acknowledge how this particular elderly man is connected to the city as such through his participation in a series of seemingly small and insignificant events taking place in distinct venues throughout the urban landscape. He moves about in an ongoing engagement with the city in order to keep busy, to obtain a salutary peace and to escape feelings of loneliness, boredom, restlessness and despair. Fieldwork has shown how he also moves to escape his self in a narrow sense of this notion, and to accompany different elements and beings of the city.

With reference to Desjarlais[17], we can observe how the two very similar words *peace* and *pace* are closely connected in this regard. How the presence on the streets, whether it is characterised by literal continuous movement or by 'moving out' of the confined residential spaces and 'moving around', roaming, loitering (cf. "Birds" example above), can lead to feelings of freedom and constitute forms of rewarding and de-individualising processes among unusual elderly people.

---

17 See excerpt on p.79.

I have accompanied Anders on his troublesome and slow walks from his second-storey room in the nursery home unit to the sidewalk where he goes to sit on the nearest street corner. Out in the open he takes his position on a newspaper depot-box in front of the street kiosk. Other inhabitants of the nursery home arrive to relieve shaking hands and bodies with remedies of alcohol and nicotine. Silences, annoyances, laughs, harsh irony, loathing, idiosyncratic and halting conversations loom in the air. Disputes arise when bodies gather. Inhabitants of the district come by, pass by, dogs dragging their humans, humans dragging their plastic bags and their gazes. City surfaces carrying them all; humans as others. The same surfaces are covering the world below, lids of the worlds below.[18] A composite superorgan in which to partake. Superorganism.[19]

I have accompanied Lars on his repetitive strides between the blocks and streets of his walking sanctuary – to the regular bar to which he returns during the day to purchase chunks of hashish, a substance of utmost importance, to the brick-recess on the main artery where he withdraws into the shadows while staying close to the currents of the city, to the sidewalk strip where he stays to receive cash donations and stretch hook-lines of spoken language into the world, lines that seem to briefly **mend the gap** between **self** and a **multitude of other**s, hooks cast and drawn – "Could you spare a coin, Mister?"

I have accompanied "Bird" as we have been sitting on shifting benches along the traffic on the main street reaching through the asphalt world. He accompanied the rays of the sun as they splashed onto the pavements and his sunburned skin, he accompanied the rhythm of the day, the traffic and the spectacles, he accompanied the city while I accompanied him; a talking, at times silent, disturbance. A friendly disturbance. We became a four-eyed gaze over time, temporarily and in passing, scrutinising the city-atmosphere, its people, its flows and its animals. Commenting on the immediate occurrences and reflecting upon their connection to distant, past and future ones – working on the endless production of memories. One day he was off the streets, gone, suddenly missing. Months later the

---

18 Rattle big black bones / In the Danger Zone / There's a rumblin' groan / Down below / There's a big dark town / It's a place I've found / There's a world going on / Underground. Tom Waits, "Underground" (1983).
19 Cf. the Dunn reference above, p.74.

nearest, although still very shallow, acquaintances reported how he had left the world, taking flight from his living room window to be found shattered on the concrete below. Left the world? Or disappeared into the world? How he **escape**d his **self** to join a **multitude of other**s.

In the work of German philosopher Walter Benjamin (2003), movement, or the sheer opportunity of being able to move about, is described as a critical factor in the lives of human beings. It is a physical as well as an intellectual prerequisite to the experience of freedom. In Paris such kinds of freedom were restricted and seriously affected when Baron Haussmann replaced the crooked and spidery streets inherent to the old city with straight-lined, broad boulevards during the 1850s (ibid.) – changes that, according to Benjamin, marked a new era of public government. Benjamin's critique has resonated in my work among the unusual elderly of Copenhagen as they all find space for dwelling and existence in different corners, routes and nooks afforded by the publicly accessible asphalt world. Furthermore, I argue, that the possibility of such 'loiter'-like[20] presence enables these people to establish, develop and maintain a dynamic relationship with the city because their practices are carried out in curious structures of movement, or as a result of such movement, as described above. The empirically based paragraphs on Anders, Lars and "Bird" provide examples of such practices. Furthermore, they articulate how these seemingly lonely people are alone as well as embedded in the city on more fundamental levels when they reside in their street dwellings; when they roam, circulate, stop, stay and move about. The descriptions point to how they all consult, enmesh and reside in their city, how they are able to engage with it in their own unusual ways, how it somehow provides for them in forms of distractions, sensations and possibilities and how it can take on the character of a companion in everyday life. In this regard the urban sphere is a field that allows for experiences of transcendence. So-called individuals are given an opportunity to step out of their confined and self-referential worlds while stepping into the city. They are given a chance to acquire company, peace and more-than-individuality in the arms, as well

---

20 Cf. the governance of public space found in metropolises as e.g. New York City where signs such as "No Loitering!", "No Hanging Out!", "No Standing Anytime!", "Private Property" and the like are prominent elements in the public and semipublic sphere. See also Robert Rosenberger's work on *callous objects* (2017) for a systematic critique of the anti-loitering designs found in urban settings.

as in the 'pockets', of the asphalt world. The city trigger affect, experiences of de-individualisation, co-existence and transcendence; it can be an embrace; constitute companionship. This kind of *being-in-the-city* can fray and challenge the constitution of the self. The practices described amplify how we as human beings are able to accompany, to be absorbed by and follow along, and to become constituent parts of larger-scale creatures and superorganisms.

The city as composite object and companion

Drawing on the American philosopher Graham Harman, the aforementioned *symbiosis* involving people as well as other components[21] can be understood as a composite object – a unit of units (e.g. Harman 2010, 2016). As Harman points out, the most ordinary conception of an object is related to entities that are lifeless, enduring, stable, non-human, or entities simply consisting of physical matter (2016, p. 40); a fork, a book, a house. Meanwhile, these examples can easily be challenged in their character of solid and bounded things; in their postulated individuality and separation from the rest of the worlds matter and material components. What is problematised here is the above-mentioned normative and taken-for-granted kind of bounded, fixed or exclusive (as in the process of exclusion) *selfhood* often ascribed to humans as well as the material and other-than-human world. We tend to understand objects like houses, books and forks as isolated and inert pieces of matter. But as is known from our ordinary engagements with the worldly environment, the house is a unit consisting of composite and easily separable objects: bricks, doors, water pipes, coffee cups, electrical wires, furniture, forks and books. Any object, whether small or of larger stature, has a composite character.[22] From the position of *object-oriented ontology*, or OOO[23], a given entity qualifies as an 'object' as soon as it is irreducible to its components and/or its effects alone – when it is something other than the 'nature' of its own material constitution and relations to given neighbouring objects.[24]

As Timothy Morton, another advocate of OOO points out, such objects can

---

21 See introduction, p. 72.
22 Cf. the teachings of basic physics dating back to ancient Greek philosophy.
23 A newer philosophical movement initiated by Graham Harman.
24 This marks the most radical break with kindred material-focused (or sensitive) philosophical endeavors as e.g. *assemblage theory* and *ANT* (see Harman, 2016, pp. 40-1, 95-114).

be of enormous range, of an extensive composite character, and due to this not necessarily fathomable for conventional forms of rational understanding, description or any kind of intentional phenomenological experience. In this context, Morton has coined the concept of 'hyperobjects' – objects of such non-local and far-reaching quality that we are not able to face them as such, as complete entities, in any form of direct phenomenological experience (Morton 2013). A good example of such a hyperobject is the city – in one sense a defined entity, in others a phenomenon, or an object, characterised by numerous constituents, elements, beings, boundaries etc. In other words: when contemplating the intellectual construction of 'the city' we piece together a certain puzzle, we exercise partially speculative acts in order to greet and conceive of this phenomenon or object as a whole. This reduction appears above in the situation involving a man engaging with wild birds in a churchyard – a situation that contains numerous constructed borders and elements that are prioritised, while others are forgotten, or omitted from the description (e.g. trees, gravestones, sound of nearby motorised traffic, insects humming, the gravel on the path, the breeze, a passer-by etc.). So-called empirical experience is limited in this regard, and the fabrication of knowledge calls for acts of speculation to fill in the gaps (see also Bergson 2014; Harman 2011). The composite object, or the *hyperobject city*, has no firm and stable identity,[25] no clear-cut boundaries – it has no distinct boundedness whatsoever – and due to this it has no exact locality that enables face-to-face encounters with the totality of this 'thing'. We can represent the city on a map (see eg. Solnit 2010; Lin 2016), display it on an aerial photograph or in other types of illustration and representation but we cannot encounter it phenomenologically.

When applying this perspective on the city, by seeing it as a composite and diffuse whole, an object consisting of both material and immaterial elements, we approach a way of grasping why the *being* of cities – cities as *creatures* and *companions* in everyday life – eludes precise description. In the analysis above, I employ the concrete parts of a situation to address a much more complex composition. As both Harman and Morton emphasise, we cannot fathom the complexity and scope of the city-object, and any attempt to narrow such beings

---

25 Cf. the etymological roots of the concept of *identity*: "Sameness, oneness, state of being the same," from Middle French *identité* (14c.), from Medieval Latin *identitatem* "sameness," ultimately from Latin *idem* "the same": www.etymonline.com/search?q=identity, accessed on February 23rd, 2021.

down to a complete representation will leave us with an even poorer understanding of their object-ness (or character) (Harman 2010, 2016; Morton 2013). The *being of cities*, these incomprehensible organisms of different lifeforms, bits, distractions, flows, lines, phenomena and temporalities are atmospheric, diffuse and non-local wholes. They are composite *per se*. As city dwellers we encounter curbstones, sidewalks, pedestrians, passages, rain, vegetation, animals, houses, drainpipes and so on. We step into this whole as participants and composite part(aker)s of (and in) its totality. But the city as such, the city as an intimate and attentive creature, an omnipresent being, a backdrop on which we lean, an atmospheric whole we are both drawn to and rejected by and to which we cling in order to remain afloat in the currents of everyday life (Ingold 2015) – this 'creature' transcends its concrete elements and constituents in all ways. It is both an embracing Mortonian hyperobject, and a companion creature to follow, engage in, part with, return to, live in and live along.

The theoretically induced notions unfolded above can assist the diffuse empirical experience of an omnipresent city-being and by drawing actively on these lines of thought it becomes possible to fathom how human and other-than-human components can cling together, weave and knot certain broad alliances in the practice of everyday life. How elderly people and other persons periodically are able to enter this totality on profound experiential levels – as absorbed partakers in an evolving whole, as movement, lines and life that flow through and merge with the city-creature while also being left on the outside as observers of the buzz. How the city-sphere can nurse, care for, accommodate, indulge and challenge the people (and other species/components) it encompasses.

Companion, companions

> "[…] the nocturnal city has been a constant, if not always coherent, companion." (Dunn 2016, p. 2)

Carl spends his days traveling and traversing the city. By bus, by train, walking. He is cautious and utterly hesitant with people, suspicious with people, but somehow safe in the arms of specific places and monuments, safe in the presence of certain areas. He likes to dwell and dream, to step into the history that paves the old streets and the quaysides of the former industrial harbour. Breathing in the moist air makes him feel at ease, sets him afloat in a weightless space. Affinity. It is not about the actual people in these places, he explains. It is not about the actual materials and monuments. It is about dwelling in a past-links-to-present atmosphere. A thread in the **fabric**.[26] Thread(s) becoming fabric. Affinity. Voices emanate from this world, form this world, if you are willing to listen, to follow along, he says. **Para-mind**. A companion city.

> "… you're fabric now … para-mind, para-mind"
> Bon Iver. "29 #Strafford APTS."

References

Adorno, T. (2005 [1951]). *Minima Moralia: Reflections from Damaged Life*. London: Verso.

Asplund, J. (1987). *Det sociala livets elementära former*. Gothenburg: Korpen.

Auster, P. (2008). *The New York Trilogy*. Los Angeles: Green Integer.

Bachelard, G. (1994). *The Poetics of Space*. Boston: Beacon Press.

Benjamin, W. (2003). *The Arcades Project* (4th printing). Cambridge: Harvard University Press.

Bergson, H. (2014). *Henri Bergson: Key Writings* (Pearson, K. A. & McMahon, M., Eds.). London: Bloomsbury Academic.

Blumer, H. (1986). *Symbolic Interactionism: Perspective and Method*. Berkeley and Los Angeles: University of California Press.

Bon Iver. (2016). *22, A Million*, track 5: 29 #Strafford APTS. Jagjaguwar.

Costandi, M. (2012). Microbes on your mind. *Scientific American Mind, 23*(3), 32-7.

Desjarlais, R. (1997). *Shelter Blues: Sanity and Selfhood among the Homeless*. Philadelphia: University of Pennsylvania Press.

Dunn, N. (2016). *Dark Matters: A Manifesto for the Nocturnal City*. Washington: Zero Books.

Ehn, B., & Löfgren, O. (2010). *The Secret World of Doing Nothing*. Berkeley: University of California Press.

---

26 This also refers to the popular metaphor of the city as an "urban fabric" (e.g. Lefebvre 2003 p. 4).

Feld, S. (1982). *Sound and Sentiment: Birds, Weeping, Poetics, and Song in Kaluli Expression*. Durham: Duke University Press.

Gilbert, S. F. (2017). Holobiont by birth: multilineage individuals as the concretion of cooperative processes. In: Tsing, A., Swanson, H., Gan, E. & Bubandt, N. (Eds.), *Arts of Living on a Damaged Planet: Monsters of the Anthropocene* (pp. 73-89). Minneapolis: University of Minnesota Press.

Haraway, D. (1988). Situated knowledges: the science question in feminism and the privilege of partial perspective. *Feminist Studies, 14*(3), 575-99.

Haraway, D. J. (2008). *When Species Meet*. Minneapolis: University of Minnesota Press.

Haraway, D. J. (2016). *Staying with the Trouble: Making Kin in the Chthulucene*. Durham: Duke University Press.

Harman, G. (2010). *Towards Speculative Realism: Essays and Lectures*. Ropley: Zero Books.

Harman, G. (2011). *The Quadruple Object*. Winchester: Zero Books.

Harman, G. (2016). *Immaterialism: Objects and social theory*.

Hede, I. M., & Kjølner Hansen, S. S. (2014). *Inferno*. Copenhagen: Arena.

Ingold, T. (2007). *Lines: A Brief History*. New York: Routledge.

Ingold, T. (2015). *The Life of Lines*. New York: Routledge.

Kohn, E. (2013). *How Forests Think: Toward an Anthropology Beyond the Human*. Berkeley: University of California Press.

Laugesen, P. (2016). *Brev til en maler*. Copenhagen: Gyldendal.

Lefebvre, H. (2003). *The Urban Revolution*. Minneapolis: University of Minnesota Press.

Lin, Shijan, (2016). *Cartographics – Designing the Modern Map*. Guangzhou: SendPoints Publishing Co.

Lund, K. (2012). Landscapes and narratives: compositions and the walking body. *Landscape Research, 37*(2), 225-37.

Mason, J. (2018). *Affinities: Potent Connections in Personal life*. Cambridge: Polity.

Morton, T. (2016). *Dark Ecology: For a Logic of Future Coexistence*. New York: Columbia University Press.

Morton, T. (2017). *Humankind: Solidarity with Nonhuman People*. London: Verso.

Morton, T. (2013). *Hyperobjects: Philosophy and Ecology after the End of the World*. Minneapolis: University of Minnesota Press.

MØ. (2018). *Forever Neverland*, track 4: Blur. Columbia Records.

Petersen, D. O. J. (2017). At the mountains of monstrosity: towards ecomonstrous entanglements through images of a fjord. *Women, Gender & Research*, *26*(2/3), 70-88.

Rasmussen, J. D. (2016 – unpublished). Den socialalkymistiske indstilling: I retning af en kreativ samfundsvidenskabelig analysepraksis.

Rasmussen, J. D. (2017a). *En upåagtet verden af bevægelse: Et etnografisk studie af hverdagsliv blandt usædvanlige ældre mennesker i storbyen*. Aalborg: Aalborg Universitetsforlag.

Rasmussen, J. D. (2017b). Urban borderlands of mobility: Ethnographic fieldwork amongst unconventional older city people. In Freudendal-Pedersen, M., Hartmann-Petersen, K. & Fjalland, E. L. P. (Eds.), *Experiencing Networked Urban Mobilities: Sites, Methods, Practices*. New York: Routledge.

Rasmussen, J. D. (2020). Movement as a practice of dwelling (p. 95) & The Empty Lot: An Urban Wilderness (p. 233). In Ly Serena, K. & Hauderowicz, D. (Eds.), *Age Inclusive Public Space*. Stuttgart: Hatje Cantz Verlag.

Rees, T., Bosch, T. & Douglas, A. E. (2018). How the microbiome challenges our concept of self. *PloS Biol. PLoS Biology*, *16*(2).

Rosenberger, R. (2017). *Callous Objects: Designs Against the Homeless*. Minneapolis: The University of Minnesota Press.

Simmel, G. (1950). The metropolis and mental life. In K. H. Wolff (Ed.), *The Sociology of Georg Simmel* (pp. 409-24). New York: Free Press.

Solnit, R. (2001). *Wanderlust: A History of Walking*. London: Verso.

Solnit, R. (2010). *Infinite City: A San Francisco Atlas*. Berkeley: University of California Press.

Strindberg, A. (2016). *The Inferno*. Jefferson Publication.

Taussig, M. (2015). *The Corn Wolf*. Chicago: University of Chicago Press.

Thoreau, H. D. (2014). *Walking: Seven Elements in Nature Writing*. Scotts Valley: CreateSpace.

Waits, T. (1983). *Swordfishtrombones,* track 1: Underground. Island Records Inc.

Whitehead, A. N. (1978). *Process and Reality: An Essay in Cosmology*. New York: Free Press.

Willerslev, R. (2007). *Soul Hunters: Hunting, Animism, and Personhood Among the Siberian Yukaghirs*. Berkeley: University of California Press.

Ørntoft, T. (2014). *Digte 2014*. Copenhagen: Gyldendal.

CHAPTER 6:

Designing place through rhythms and affinities

Anne-Lene Sand

Introduction

I opened the door to Hal12, the local skateboarding hall in Roskilde, and the silence hit me; where were the familiar sounds of skateboard wheels crossing ramps, pipes and pavement and boards slamming onto the pavement? Was no-one skating? That particular day, Hal12 was closed to the regular users and skateboarders. Only people with wheelchairs could participate. I was only allowed to observe the event Street on Wheels if I participated in a wheelchair like the other practitioners[1]. That suited me very well due to my anthropological approach to understanding embodied practices and my memories of spinning on rear wheels in informal wheelchair competitions during high school. I met Bo, one of the organisers of the Street on Wheels event, and he directed me towards a helmet and wheelchair equipment I could borrow. I felt a bit of adrenaline running through my arms and stomach as I rolled into the hall. A huge landscape of classical skateboarding architecture was lined up as permanent installations in the centre of the hall. As I sat in my chair, one metre high, the physical installations seemed huge. The tricks I had learned for fun as a youngster suddenly seemed far away, and I felt humble in comparison to the other wheelchair practitioners. I passed a few people standing on their feet and several people in wheelchairs along the sides of the hall, and I positioned myself sitting alongside the other practitioners – out there, on the floor. In total, I counted around 30 wheelchairs. Hesitating, we waited. We heard metal (from a wheelchair) hit a pipe, which broke the silence. We turned our wheels, and David Lebuser, a professional German wheelchair skater who had been invited to run the workshop, arrived. He

---

1   Introduction video (2015). https://vimeo.com/135949589

drove fast down a ramp and slid down a pipe in his chair. At this moment, the adrenaline took on the character of discomfort in my body. Was I going to do that? The other wheelchair users seemed out of their element too, as they had difficulty making eye contact with each other and Lebuser and were looking down. In front of us we had a whole day of exploring the new constellation between the chair, bodies and the material environment. (Fieldnotes, December 2014)

Figure 1: David Lebuser illustrating Sit n' skate.

In 2015-2018 I was carrying out a research project whose aim was to generate knowledge about the organisation of alternative cultures of movement, such as skateboarding, parkour, street soccer and more alternative forms like urban climbing and Sit n' skate. I followed projects which had gained financial support from the National Platform for Street Sports (http://gadeidraet.dk/). The fieldwork was characterised as a multi-sited (Hannerz 2003), short and focused ethnographic fieldwork (Pink & Morgan 2013)[2]. Throughout this chapter, I draw on empirical material from the event Street on Wheels, which was centred on the practice Sit n' Skate. The empirical material nuances how a traditional skateboarding hall was transformed into a place for wheelchair practitioners where they could experience, explore and exceed embodied practices in skateboarding facilities while using their wheelchairs. The event Street on Wheels was organised on the initiative of two men; Bo, who was the leader of an existing skate hall, and Jesper, who is a wheelchair user himself. The idea was to introduce Sit n' Skate to Danish wheelchair users by making a playful space where wheelchair users could have fun and get experienced with new types of movement between body, chair and skate facilities. Bo and Jesper wanted to make a safe place where wheelchair users were the majority of people

---

2   This research project was funded by the Carlsberg Foundation.

skating. I was allowed to participate as a researcher, but only if I participated in a wheelchair. From the perspective of a chair, although for only the one day the event took place, I observed and participated in the challenges held during the event. It allowed me to reflect on how designing place to a large extent is sensory and socially embedded, which from a design anthropological perspective raises questions about future design of place. Furthermore, it made me reflect on how transforming place through a participatory and dynamic design process can provide alternative embodied experiences for wheelchair users. Being positioned as a researcher in a one-metre-high chair with wheels constructed a comparative dialogue between apparently skilled wheelchair practitioners and me, as a novice, and at the same time, brought me into an overwhelming landscape of architectural installations.

Within this chapter, place is understood as the embodied, material and physical dimensions of place and the notion of space refers to the spatial, temporal, social and cultural dimensions (Cresswell 2004). A sensitive approach to place is necessary in order to understand the dynamic and sensory character of place and to reflect how a design of places can accommodate these dimensions (Nyseth, Førde and Cruickshank 2018). Design has often been understood as a product development related to specific problem-solving, but the field of design has developed into more dynamic design processes (Brown and Martin 2015). A newer approach within design is design anthropology, which as a discipline has been developed to a particular degree in Denmark (Smith, Vangkilde, Otto, Halse and Binder 2016; Gunn, Otto and Smith 2013; Brandt, Messeter and Binder 2008). Design anthropology makes an important contribution to design thinking since it has everyday life as epistemological departure: "Practitioners of design anthropology follow dynamic situations and social relations and are concerned with how people perceive, create, and transform their environments through their everyday activities." (Gunn, Otto and Smith 2013, p. xiii). As argued, design anthropology is about learning through dynamic and social relations and taking seriously the way in which people influence their environment in everyday situations. In contrast to being a descriptive and analytical discipline, the concept of *future* brings forth a design anthropological interest in change and future-making (ibid., p. 10), which Joachim Halse describes as 'ethnographies of the possible' (Halse 2018, p. 180). The aim of this chapter is not to contribute a design solution, but instead raise questions of design anthropological relevance and reflect upon how affinities and rhythms are a part of the design of place. Additionally, it will shed light on how designing place for one day can provide an in-between space where people live multiple sensory experiences – individually and together. As illustrated in this chapter, making Street on Wheels was not just a question of lending a place to wheelchair users, but rather taking multiple sensitive placemaking aspects into consideration.

Theoretically, this chapter is inspired by French urban philosopher Henri Lefebvre's *Rhythmanalysis* (2004), which is discussed and developed through sociologist Jennifer Mason's (2018) concept of 'affinities'. An essential ambition in this work of Mason is to push the boundaries of sociological knowledge through a more open, attentive, inventive and sociological sensibility. Combining these theoretical perspectives makes it possible to grasp sensory practices that are processual, dynamic and improvisational, which are dimensions important to include when planning and designing place (see Pløger, Førde og Sand, 2021).

The theoretical combination of rhythms and affinities lays out a sensitive understanding of the connection between the design of place and embodied experiences of wheelchair users. Hereby, the chapter wedges *in-between* the everyday life of the skate hall and the everyday life of wheelchair users, providing a space where bodies, materiality, sociality and spatial rules are combined in new ways. The design anthropological reflections open up an in-between space between the present and the future. In other words, the event Street on Wheels and specific sit n' skate practices connect to reflections of future design of place.

The chapter consists of three analytical sections. First, *Transforming Place* analyses how the skate hall was designed through specific rules and initiatives in order to make the participants feel good about exploring the physical landscape of the skate hall in their wheelchair. Second, *Connections between everyday life, bodies and materiality* unfolds how rhythms and affinities are related to the use of materiality. Third, *Affinities connecting the individual and social* analyses how designing place also happened during the day through the way in which people in collaboration helped each other, encouraged each other and at the same time confronted their own limits of fear. All three sections give insight into how a design of the skate hall during the event was set up before and during the event and how affinities and rhythms were a part of it.

Rhythms and affinities

Henri Lefebvre and his wife Catherine Régulier introduced the concept of rhythmanalysis in 1985 (Lefebvre 2004; Lefebvre & Régulier 1985, 1986). As a neo-Marxist philosopher, inspired by Nietzsche's Dionysian perspective (Lefebvre

1991, p. 22-4) and Merleau-Ponty's phenomenology (Lefebvre 2004), Lefebvre critically advocated for legitimising alternative and playful practices. Studying everyday life in Paris, Lefebvre (2004) noticed different types of movements: people walking, crossing the street, shopping and playing music; cars accelerating; and different formations of people, smells and sounds. He observed routine temporalities and how the clock marked certain times and actions, such as lunch breaks and school opening and dismissal (Lefebvre 1987, p. 31). Lefebvre wrote that 'everywhere there is interaction between a place, a time, and an input of energy; there is rhythm' (Lefebvre, 2004, p. 15, original emphasis). Lefebvre did not provide a clear definition of *rhythm*, but argued that rhythms are everywhere and an embedded part of social life. The strength of this framework is that it attempts to understand rhythms through a perspective of temporality, and seeing different dimensions of practice as temporal, which makes it possible to combine, compare and discuss dimensions of practice that are related, even though they are very different.

Lefebvre passed away in 1991 and left the conceptual framework of rhythmanalysis somewhat unfinished. In my previous work I have illustrated how the rhythmanalysis has potential for further development. I developed the concept of *a spatial jam session*, which provides a framework suitable for analysing spatial dimension of contemporary youth culture (Sand 2017). Using the concept of *a spatial jam session*, I argue that a central aspect of young people's placemaking is being able to improvise with what I analyse as rhythms of material, social and cultural character. Within this chapter I will illustrate how Mason's concept of affinities can supplement the concept of rhythmanalysis and gain more detailed insight in sensory practices which are ad hoc, improvisatorial, dynamic and processual.

Despite the great potential of Lefebvre's (2004) rhythmanalysis, the conceptual framework becomes limited when dealing with different types of senses. Lefebvre characterised different types of rhythms but he did not apply the concepts at a practice level, which leaves it on one hand categorical, but on the other hand interesting to develop in relation to everyday practices. For example, in my previous work, I analysed how young people developed their own practices of improvisation, which included applying different types of urban rhythms (Sand 2017). Even though Lefebvre categorises rhythms into four types (to which I will return shortly), I argue that Mason's concept of affinity can help analyse sensory dimensions that are difficult to grasp and capture analytically as energies, flows, forces and charges. These dimensions are not mentioned nor articulated in the theory of rhythmanalysis. Although the concept of affinities can seem somewhat difficult to grasp, Mason develops a sensory-kinaesthetic attunement, aimed at recognising that interactions are full of sensory information and kinesthetics which come together in what Mason describes as 'sensations' (Mason 2018, p. 7). "To begin with I mean that sensations are not simply derived from single sensory stimuli, or perceived through singular sensory receptors, for example, of sight, touch, smell. It is helpful here to reiterate the difference in definitions of 'senses' and 'sensations'." (Mason 2018, pp. 42-3). Sensations are different senses which are rolled together in the mutual and relational experience of sensations. According to Mason, sensations are manifest and of interest in themselves; they do not simply stand for, tell us about or express something else (ibid., p. 46). Thereby Mason argues that sensations call for analytical attention, and deserve it in themselves, instead of rushing too quickly towards abstracted interpretations (ibid., p. 47). Within a sensation, connections can be triggered or evoked, which makes them potent – as power, energy or sparks, that bring forth strong emotions. This is 'affinities' (ibid., pp. 47-8), potent connections that rise up and matter (ibid., p. 1).

Looking at Lefebvre's framework, rhythms can connect differently, and Lefebvre categorizes them into four types of rhythmic connectedness: *polyrhythmia, isorhythmia, eurhythmia* and *arrhythmia*. Polyrhythmia refers to rhythms that co-exist with no mutual conflict. Isorhythms form a co-ordinated, hierarchical positioning of rhythms. Eurhythmia refers to visible rhythms that are harmonic to each other. Arrhythmia denotes rhythms in conflict or discord with each other (Lefebvre 2004, p. 68). Within this chapter I will draw explicitly on *eurhythmia* and *arrhythmia*, since they bring forth an understanding of how sensory dimensions can be constructive or conflicting and might trigger different kinds of affinities in different people. Other rhythms will be introduced throughout the chapter.

Rhythms and affinities provide a foundation for understanding how designing place isn't just about changing a physical environment or changing the social rules for places. It is also about different kinds of rhythms and complex sensations, which are filled with sparks, energies and flows (i.e. affinities) (cf. Mason 2018, p. 86). Combining Lefebvre's and Mason's perspectives on different types of sensory practices forces us to think differently by trying to grasp phenomenon in everyday practices that are slippery, instant and improvisatorial. These are sensitive dimensions that are rarely taken into consideration in specific design- and plan processes (see Pløger, Førde and Sand 2021). Rhythms and affinities nuance how transforming place did more than provide an inclusive place for wheelchair users: it also generated a place that maintained sensory possibilities and exceeded boundaries of the body, surpassing and handling affinities and emotions related to excitement and fear.

1. Designing place

I interviewed Kasper, who had been skating for more than 30 years, and he explained how specific rules dominated the practices in skateboarding halls. For example, the existing social norms prescribed that, if scooter users were welcome, they ranked lower hierarchically than people who skateboarded, which influenced the space they could occupy. The social relationships among skateboarders were also highly competitive and hierarchical and certain styles dominated skateboarding culture. Bo, who arranged Street on Wheels, explained that he wanted to change the normal use of the skate hall and make a temporary design where wheelchair users could enjoy bodily experiences in alternative ways through movement with their chairs, and perhaps generate new ideas of what they were physically capable of. For example, Bo and Jesper, the two initiators, closed Hal12 to skateboarders and allowed only wheelchair users to participate in order to make it possible for the wheelchair users to challenge embodied logics of what they could and should do in their chairs. For Bo, designing place in this way was also about constructing a space where they felt safe to skate. He explained:

> *Several of [the wheelchair users] were afraid of falling in their chairs, which is understandable. Arranging the event, we talked a lot about how to normalise the practice of falling. A video was made from last year's event, and they cut out all the sequences where people actually fell. We asked them to maintain that specific aspect in the video in order to normalise the aspect of falling. It is okay if it looks a bit dangerous. By showing when people fall out of their chairs, we legitimise it. When skateboarding, we have to make it legitimate to fall.* (Interview, January 2016)

An essential aim of the event was to create a place suitable and comfortable for wheelchair users. The empirical example illustrates that redefining place was not only about changing the formal, temporal and spatial structures of place but also transforming and playing with feelings of being in place. Drawing upon Lefebvre we can begin to articulate and understand how Bo designs a place, by making explicit rules about participation, allowing few audience members and journalists to observe, communicating through a video, constructing an image of mild danger in order to legitimise the risk of falling, considering feelings like fear and how to design a safe place where wheelchair users can challenge themselves. All these dimensions, which are connected, can be understood as rhythms (since they all have a temporal extent) being coordinated in order to generate a certain type of eurhythmic rhythm which, according to Lefebvre, are connected in a harmonic way. As I will illustrate later, the coordination of rhythms is important since it will influence the sensory experience of the participants.

During the event, Bo closes the hall for skateboarders. Everyday life has linear rhythms, where the repetition of practices is essential (Lefebvre 2004). As illustrated above, Bo changed the everyday linear rhythm of Hal12 and created a playful place. Lefebvre uses the concept of cyclical rhythms to describe how a determined period can foster alternative and playful sensory experiences (Lefebvre 2004, p. 90). Changing the everyday linearity of Hal12 created a cyclical space where the practitioners could exceed and challenge themselves, their chairs and the materiality of the physical environment. This nuances how place can be designed through situating sensitive and sensory experiences – letting different rhythms generate new embodied experiences and letting the practitioners exceed embodied boundaries.

According to Lefebvre, rhythms can be represented without being present (Lefebvre 1996, p. 223 in: Amin and Thrift 2002, p. 17); for example, internal rhythms are expressed within the body as feelings or sensory experiences. According to Bo, communicating the event through a video influences the practitioners' expectations and what it physically requires of them, and minimises the fear of falling. This nuances how the process of designing places can be related to sensitive dimensions such as feelings. Another element of transforming place was that the wheelchair practitioners were allowed to bring their helpers who supported them in everyday life to minimise potential fear. Furthermore, two men without chairs were invited to support the practitioners as they tried some of the challenges, catching them if they fell and simply being beside them as they rode. By inviting helpers, Bo set up a design that was connected to a safe place to practice sit n' skate, which might have encouraged the practitioners to try new challenging exercises.

One aspect of designing place is organising and planning how it will be used and what might happen. But not least, places take shape through social and embodied practices. In the following, I aim to illustrate how the exercises the practitioners were encouraged to try out were connected to the design of the physical environment, and generated rhythms and affinities based on fear and excitement.

2. Connections between everyday life, bodies and materiality

Several exercises at Street on Wheels took place outside Hal12 at the architectural site Rabalderparken[3] (Figure 2), a park combining facilities for skateboarding and rainwater containment. As we drove along a path to a bigger ramp, we could as practitioners choose to either drive down four or five stairs, designed for walking, or along a zig-zag slide, designed for wheels, which was a bit longer.

Figure 2: Hal12, Street on Wheels 2015, with practitioners in wheelchairs, a few helpers and a camera crew documenting the workshop. Photo by the author.

---

3   Rabalderparken (http://www.snearchitects.com/project/rabalderparken/) is a large park with drainage canals and water reservoirs collecting rainwater from adjacent areas of the city. The overall theme of the park is celebration of free movement and the flow of water.

In-between. Exploring cracks of everyday life

The two paths were a challenge to me; they made me want to explore. I wanted to drive down the stairs, not because the path was shorter, but because the sharp edges of the vertical stairs sparked curiosity in me. Relating this to Mason's concept of affinity, the connection between the stairs, my manoeuvring a wheelchair, and the spatial setup, which was designed to allow exploration of new ways of driving within a safe environment, evoked an eagerness that was rooted in my way of adapting to the physical landscape. It made my fingers itch, so to speak, in order to grab the wheel, drive and try it out. I wanted to experience whether I could manage the task with my body. From my standpoint, the different sensory dimensions concurred, which from a rhythm analytical perspective can be described as a eurhythmic and harmonic connectedness. During the day all of us in a wheel chair talked about the environment and the tasks we had to do. At one point Casper who is a 10-year-old boy in a wheelchair, and I are both looking at the stairs in front of us and I ask him: "Have you tried to drive down the stairs? Is there a special technique?" "I don't know," Casper answered, quickly turning away from me in his wheelchair. After this short dialogue, I wondered why he did not know. Participating in the event as a novice, I felt curious about the physical environment. I wanted to explore and challenge what I could do in the chair in the specific physical environment.

Figure 3: Casper trying to ride without the stick. Photo: Bo.

Figure 3 shows me balancing on the rear wheels of a chair and Figure 4 shows Casper driving at the end of a ramp. I sensed and observed that Casper and the other participants were more oriented towards what they could not do than what they could do. I was trying to understand the different approaches we had to the physical environment. My experience within that specific environment and approach to the challenges of the day exhibited as 'itchy fingers' and a curiosity towards the physical environment, which seemed to increase my courage. Mason describes affinities as "sparks or charges of connection that intensify, enchant or indeed toxify personal life and the experience of living" (Mason 2018, p. 186). What Mason describes as affinities can be used to understand how the place came together through multisensory dimensions, such as the challenges, the chair, material obstacles to pass and so forth. Observations and dialogues with Casper indicated that he experienced it somewhat differently and did not feel the same eagerness to explore the physicality of, for example, the stairs. Why? Most of the practitioners had been in chairs for several years. In my eyes, they were everyday professionals, but what did I not see at that point?

The situation described above raises questions about what made the difference between what I experienced and my observations of Casper's reaction. Mason's perspective helps us come to an understanding:

> *Affinities are experienced as particularly potent connections with specific others who are characters with appearances, smells, voice, gestures, physicality, habits … ways of being in the world, traits, political and moral orientations and, of course, their own personal socio-cultural relational histories. It is the particularities of character and the role of characters-in-relation.* (Mason 2018, p. 51)

Reading Mason's book, it becomes clear that essential parts of affinities are related to the past and what she here calls socio-cultural relational histories. I tried to understand the specific situation – the body, the wheelchair and the physical environment – and how we brought together different backgrounds and positions to Street on Wheels. For example, my role as a researcher doing sensory emplaced participation (cf. Pink 2008) became a kind of an explorative, relatively fun activity as I was able to stand up and walk out when the event was over. What I experienced could be described as affinities related to cyclical rhythms, as it was temporally short and experienced as primarily playful, and nowhere related to my everyday life.

Casper and the other wheelchair users were playful too, but their position was connected to their everyday practices (linear rhythms) where they had to exceed habituated everyday practices of going about their everyday lives in a wheelchair – not as someone who was riding on the back of the wheels of a wheelchair in high school, but as someone who would always be in a chair. These different everyday backgrounds and roles can help understand how the complex interplay of everyday practices, the particular play, the chairs, bodies, materiality and so forth generate sensations that spark affinities and give insights into glimpse of emotions like anxiety, hesitation, courage, eagerness and playfulness.

At the event, Casper was the only one his age. His father and mother attended with him, and they often spoke intimately together. Casper seemed shy and distanced himself from the other participants during the day. He drove faster than the others, and accelerating and speeding seemed to be playful ways in which he used his wheelchair. All the participants had their own personalised chairs, and I observed that Casper's chair differed from the others due to a metal stick pointing backwards a few centimetres from the ground. In Casper's everyday life, the function of the stick was connected to feelings of safety in order to stop the chair if it got off balance and tipped backwards. At this event, the stick seemed to foster feelings other than safety. Bo told me that, while the stick seemed to be a corporate part of Casper's embodied everyday practices, during the event it limited Casper's exploration of the physical environment. Elaborating on this analytical point means that skating with a stick before the event secured the interplay between body and materiality. In Lefebvre's terminology, the way in which the stick, the body and environment work together demonstrate a harmonic and eurhythmic interplay (Lefebvre 2004, p. 68). But in contrast, transforming the place into what Bo describes as a 'safe place for skating', where the practitioners could explore and exceed what they were capable of, the stick seemed limiting and a boundary to the principal intentions of the event. I observed Casper throughout the day. After several hours of skating, an instructor encouraged him to remove the stick. The instructor spoke to Casper's parents, who seemed uneasy with the suggestion but ended up removing the 30 cm of materiality attached to this chair he had been driving his whole childhood.

Mason (2018) argues that affinities should not be interpreted as relational or symbolic but viewed as sparks that set loose an energy or force that might limit or push a person. Early in the day, the experience Casper seemed to be searching for consisted of driving really fast and experiencing uncertainty while gaining familiarity with the surfaces of the physical environment, the wheelchair and his body. An hour after removing the stick, Casper overcame obstacles he had not attempted earlier that day. He was fast before, but now he used different techniques, such as lifting the front wheels of the chair off the ground. Practices that previously created conflict now seemed to be different and to be constructively related since he rode differently and explored the physical environment in a more curious and playful way. I observed the look on Casper's face and he seemed excited and revealed an expression of 'look what I can do'. His lips slightly pressed together in a careful smile, he seemed happy and said: "It's been fun. I have never had the guts to drive down something before." He then took off again, accelerating fast, his arms moved fast cross the handle on the wheels of the chair – he is just going fast while smiling.

Returning to the question of how place can be designed through rhythms of affinities, it nuances how design processes involve more than changing opening hours and social rules of the place. These sensory 'slippery' phenomena emphasise how designing place is to a large extent a social process about connections taking places *in situ*.

3. Affinities connecting the individual and the social

We just started the workshop. We line up one by one inside Hal12. We drive up a two-metre-high ramp, turn and drive back down. It isn't steep, but challenging to turn the chair while moving, without stopping. It is my turn. Hesitating, my body tells me 'no', I notice the crowd of people surrounding me, on the floor and alongside the hall. I choose not to listen to my body and I force myself to take off. And as I come up, I realize I drove too vertically. I have difficulty turning to ride down again. I cannot make it, and I turn my wheels horizontally on the ramp, and fall backwards, the chair is heavy and makes me fall hard and roll on my neck. I feel pain. From the others behind me, I hear shouts of 'Arghhh', 'Ouch'. (Fieldnotes, December 2015)

After the crash, several practitioners asked me if I was okay, which made me reflect on the situation. From the spontaneous and slightly fearful shouts I understood that I had experienced something they associated with fear: the fear of falling in a wheelchair, being hurt and unable to get up again. The entire social design was set up to minimise and at the same time confront the fear of falling in order to explore new ways of using the wheelchair. As a novice with the ability to get up on my own feet, sensing the social space that surrounded me, asking myself the question 'What do I have to lose?' and observing the others' reactions as I fell made me sense the sensitive boundaries of the social space I occupied.

During a session outside Hal12, I observed the following:

> *One woman sits in her chair up on the top of a ramp and hesitates as she is about to take off and drive down. She has seen others do the same. She laughs nervously, and one of the helpers approaches her, ready to support her when she drives down. She shouts 'Yay!' as she manages to ride down, and the other practitioners clap collectively and yell, 'Well done', 'Respect'.* (Fieldnotes, December 2015)

To Mason (2018), affinities take shape in the in-between of an interplay of multiple sensations. The frisson described above – the woman sitting positioned high on a ramp, surrounded by people ready to catch her, exploring within a specific social-relational space – generated a courage and an eagerness to exceed embodied logics. In Lefebvre's (2004) terminology, the interplay of external rhythms (material, architectural and structural), internal rhythms (embodied, sensitive and emotional) and eurhythmic rhythms (the coordination of the present rhythms) brings forth a social force, an affinity, that gave rise to the courage to ride and support each other.

The event was organised by dividing the participants into two groups. One group started in the skateboarding hall, while the other group used the skateboarding facilities outside Hal12. After two hours of practice inside the hall, a lunch break was held, with food provided for everyone. Next came a two-hour outdoor session, with more skateboarding activities such as riding down steep passages etc. We ate lunch together, a woman had a birthday and we celebrated with cake and singing and finally at the end of the day, all the participants were invited to dinner and a party with music. Transforming the skate hall, only allowing wheelchair users to participate, situated the practitioners in the same situation, which evoked a connection between then and gave them a social force. This force was observable in the ways that the participants helped and encouraged each other to try new, embodied practices together throughout the day.

At the same time, however, several rhythms constructed the contrary effect. Bo invited David Lebuser, a professional sit n' skater, to inspire the practitioners and demonstrate how wheelchairs could be used differently. Sit n' skate is a term used to describe the specific style of skating in a wheelchair. Lebuser's approach to skating is illustrated in his Instagram account through photographs and hashtags such as #fail, #sitnskate and #destroystereotypes. These hashtags emphasised that failing was part of practice, connected to pushing the boundaries of the body, the wheelchair and the material environment. Showing how to practice sit 'n skate, Lebuser became a role model for how being disabled and driving a wheelchair could bring forth new playful, embodied potentials. Potentials which are not associated with the limitations related to a wheelchair, but potentials reinforced by the ability to play, move differently, be excited, overcome fear, be challenged playfully and experience being able to do what no one ever thought of doing. Moreover, he became a model of handling fear as he continually challenged the boundaries of what he could do with his wheelchair and thus influenced the process of transforming the place. Mason argues:

> *Affinities, then, come alive in sensations. They are energies, forces and flows that can take shape in an ineffable kinship as well as in ecologies and the socio-atmospheric of life, and they articulate and resonate with time and with their times. Their potency can come from the frissons, charges, alluring discordances and poetics that animate and enliven everyday personal lives.*
> (Mason 2018, p. 200)

The potency of an affinity is expressed as different types of frissons, charges or dissonances. Designing a temporal place for wheelchair users to practise sit n' skate struck a balance between constructing a safe place where rhythms operated harmonically together and inspiring and socially encouraging the practitioners out of their embodied comfort zones. In the preceding excerpt, the female skater shouted 'Yay!' while driving off the ramp and the others shouted 'ouch' and 'arghhh'. 'Yay', 'ouch', 'arghhh' become examples of affinities confronting the challenges and transitions she, they, we and I faced during the specific day. Rhythms of arrhythmia can bring forth affinities of fear, discomfort and anxiety. In this case, the social dimensions for the design were of particular importance to the event, since it reinforced the practitioners' embodied attitudes towards the challenges they confronted during the day.

Conclusion

From the perspective of a chair, although for only the one day, I observed and participated in the event Street on Wheels and the challenges set up for wheelchair users in a skateboarding hall. My participation in a wheelchair allowed me to make design anthropological reflections and in the spirit of this anthology, open up an in-between space to bring forth reflections between the present and the future. The previous pages reveal complex layers of designing place and how re-designing places temporarily can provide embodied potentials for example wheelchairs users. The aim of the chapter has been to understand how designing place for one day can provide an in-between space wherein people experience multiple sensory experiences – individually and together.

Theoretically, this chapter draws upon Lefebvre's (2004) *Rhythmanalysis*, which is discussed and developed through sociologist Mason's (2018) concept of "affinities". Lefebvre (2004) helps us understand how places can consist of rhythms operating differently and influence everyday practices, and how place can consist of rhythms of materiality, sociality and spatiality. Through the concept of affinities, Mason's work is centred around sparks, flows and charges of connections, which reveals how elements of designing place can have a more ephemeral and improvisational character. The event Sit 'n Skate is an example of how a design can be defined in flexible terms, which allows for the participants to define the content of place as they go along. This raises design anthropological questions related to future notions of designing place; how are we to provide places of *in-between*, where the concept can be shaped through people with alternative ideas and approaches?

The three analytical parts of the chapter illustrate how designing place is about the connectedness of rhythms and how different types of connections generate different affinities. First of all, designing place for wheelchair users to explore extends beyond materiality and structure and is to a large extent about designing a safe place for embodied practices. Secondly, designing an in-between place for wheelchair users to explore is also about understanding the everyday life of wheelchair users and how unnoticeable types of materiality generate affinities, which influence feelings such as joy, hesitation, courage, fear and discomfort. Thirdly, the practices carried out during the day depended on the social connections among the practitioners, which made them encourage each other. The chapter illustrates how rhythms, sparks, flows and social forces are underlying in-between dimensions of place, which, even though they can be difficult to grasp, are important in our understanding of place. In a broader perspective, designing places for only one day is interesting since it can bring forth a discussion about how places can be designed temporarily, and create alternative sensory experiences and participatory spaces.

Because this anthology has taken seriously the 'small cracks of everyday life', I have had the opportunity to dive into an in-between workspace where I could first of all take seriously empirical material from a single day's fieldwork, and secondly explore new connections between theoretical concepts and disciplines. Thus, this chapter is a starting point for new research perspectives within my research.

References

Amin, A. & Thrift, N. (2002). *Cities: Reimagining the Urban,* Cambridge, Polity.

Brandt, E., Messeter, J., & Binder, T. (2008). Formating design dialogues: games and participation, *CoDesign*, 4 (1), 51-64.

Brown, T. & Martin, R. L. (2015). Design for action. *Harvard Business Review*, 93 (9), 57-64.

Cresswell, T. (2004). *A Short Introduction to Place*. Blackwell Publishing.

Halse, J. (2018). Ethnographies of the possible. In Gunn, W., Otto, T. and Smith, R. C. (Eds.), *Design Anthropology. Theory and Practice* (pp. 180-98). London: Bloomsbury.

Hannerz, U. (2003). Being there … and there … and there! *Ethnography,* 4 (2), 201-16.

Lefebvre, H. (1987). An interview with Lefebvre. *Environment and Planning D: Society and Space,* 5, 27-38.

Lefebvre, H. (1991). *The Production of Space,* Malden, MA, Blackwell.

Lefebvre, H. (1996). *Writings on Cities,* Oxford, Blackwell.

Lefebvre, H. (2004). *Rhythmanalysis: Space, Time and Everyday Life,* London, Continuum.

Lefebvre, H. & Régulier, C. (1985). Le projet rythmanalytique. *Communications,* 41, 191-9.

Lefebvre, H. & Régulier, C. (1986). Essai de rythmanalyse des villes méditerranéennes. *Peuples Méditerranéens,* 37, 5-16.

Mason, J. (2018). *Affinities. Potent Connections in Personal Life,* Cambridge, Polity.

Nyseth, T., Førde, A. & Cruickshank, J. (2018). Fra attraktive steder til omtenksom by- og stedsutvikling. Implikasjoner for planlegging? In Aarsæther, N., Falleth,

E., Kristiansen, R. & Nyseth, T. (Eds.), *Plan og Samfunn. System, praksis, teori* (pp. 267-285). Oslo: Cappelen Damm Akademisk.

Otto, T., & Smith, R. C. (2013). Design anthropology: A distinct style of knowing. In Gunn, W., Otto, T. & Smith, R. C. (Eds.), *Design Anthropology. Theory and Practice* (pp. 1-32). London: Bloomsbury.

Pink, S. & Morgan, J. (2013). Short-term ethnography: intense routes to knowing. *Symbolic Interaction,* 36, 351-61.

Pink, S. (2008). An urban tour. The sensory sociality of ethnographic place-making. *Ethnography* 9 (2): 175-196.

Pløger, J., Førde, A. & Sand, A-L. (2021). *Improvisation – byliv mellem planlægning og planløshed.* Oslo: Spartacus. (in press).

Sand, A-L. (2017). Jamming with urban rhythms: improvisatorial place-making among Danish youth. *Young,* 25 (3), 286-304.

CHAPTER 7:

The house: being, seeing, remembering place

Ida Wentzel Winther

In this text, I use one specific house as my jumping-off point: a large red-brick house – an old school – built in 1927, where four generations of my family have lived or spent leisure time since 1940. Fundamentally, my approach suggests that we carry the grammar of a place and a landscape within us, inscribed and stored through narratives over generations. With this in mind, I am interested in how a place is remembered perceptually, how bodily experiences are felt, initiated and ignited with a house as a catalyst. I allow the house and the landscape to hone and attune me – affect me – as I write about the interplay between the material and immaterial aspects of inhabiting this particular place. Moreover, I write in a kind of pocket – the in-between space – that may arise when the past, the present and the future are combined during a trip down memory lane. I let the memory occur between the specific house – located in a specific region, landscape and with a particular family history attached – and me as a writer.

For the past 25 years, I have written about home, Heimat, belonging and place (Winther 1996, 2006, 2009, 2016), trying to develop phenomenological research methods where I walk (both physically and theoretically) in the field (2006, 2018), and using my embedded and auto-ethnographical body as a research tool (2013). This particular study started in 2008. With great passion, I read David MacDougall's book (2006) about schoolscapes and the corporeal image, where the visual is a way to see (a specific gaze), the senses are a way to be, and the social-aesthetic environment in a school building (the schoolscape) has a language with its own vocabulary and potential. I started to listen, smell and taste more systematically, inspired by Steven Feld and Keith Basso's (1996) acoustemology of place and Murray R. Schafer's (1977) focus on our sonic environment in the world. I stationed myself in my private schoolscape – my holiday home – and tried to learn to listen as a research strategy. For hours, I sat listening to the wind, to the sound of children cycling by on their way to school, to passing cars. At the same time, the book *Ways of Walking. Ethnogra-*

phy and Practice on Foot (2008), edited by Tim Ingold & Jo Lee Vergunst, was published. It was about different senses of landscape: the landscape of earth, fields, pastures, countryside, ground and the experience of scenic space. In this book, Kenneth Olwig described two different senses of landscape:

> *The first involves binocular vision, movement, and knowledge gained from a coordinated use of the senses in carrying out various tasks (Ingold 1993). The second derives primarily from a monocular perspective that is fixed and distant from the body. The first modality engenders a sense of belonging that generates landscape as the place of dwelling, practice, and doing in the body politic of a community, whereas the second constructs a feeling of possession and staged performance in a hierarchical social space.* (2008, p. 81)

These two different senses of landscape are linked to two different ways of seeing and 'practising' landscape. With Olwig's concepts of perambulatory practice in my pocket, I headed to the coast of the North Sea, close to my house. Here, I listened to the waves, smelt and felt the windblown sand. I started to take systematic notes, focusing on the sensations of this specific place and letting the landscape put me in the mood, observing and writing about what different atmospheres do rather than what they are (Frykman 2016, p. 10). As such, this text is based on auto-ethnography, but instead of the ethnographic 'I' (Ellis 2003), I am inspired by Kathleen Stewart's (2007) way of working with a transformation of the first-person author 'I' to a third-person 'she'. To quote Stewart:

> *I call myself "she" to mark the difference between this writerly identity and the kind of subject that arises as a daydream of simple presence. "She" is not so much a subject position or an agent in hot pursuit of something definitive as a point of contact; instead, she gazes, imagines, senses, takes on, performs, and asserts not a flat and finished truth but some possibilities (and threats) that have come into view in the effort to become attuned to what a particular scene might offer.* (2007, p. 5)

I will use this method of placing the subject in writing and call myself 'she' or 'her'. From a third-person perspective, it is possible to move between layers of personal, family, local and historical details and my own private embodied knowledge. The she/her can mix and reassemble memories and narratives. Theoretically, I am informed by three different concepts, all of which circle the relationship between materiality, memory and place: ordinary affects (Stewart 2007), sensitive objects (Frykman & Frykman 2016; Löfgren 2016) and evocative objects (Turkle 2007). The text will follow several tracks: it is about arrival, departure and bidding farewell. About being attached and bonded to landscape and schoolscape (MacDougall 2006; Olwig 2008). It is about family memories and local and historical details. Fragments about being, seeing and remembering place.

****

Flat, flatter and flatter still

She is far from the metropolis. We are in the rural fringes of Denmark and by Danish standards it is a long journey to get here. She travels through the country. There are always queues heading south out of Copenhagen, strong winds across the Great Belt and heavy traffic in West Funen. Around the town Givskud, the traffic thins out, and Herning flies by. Aulum, Holstebro – trucks carrying soldiers, perhaps lost on their way to or from the local barracks. Then the landscape becomes flat, flatter and flatter still. The horizon is visible whichever way you turn. There is no end in sight; it is like expanding your lungs, and she breathes differently. The extensive landscape, an endless endlessness. At one and the same time she feels extended and she gains a pivotal sense of belonging.

Like many other small villages in the region, the village of her destination seems rather empty. Dozens of 'for sale' signs. Just one grocery store has survived, with a number of local residents working here as volunteers in an attempt to stave off the threat of closure. When she was a child in the 1970s, there were two grocers, a bakery and a dairy. She knows that in the 1940s and 60s the village also had a butcher, a fishmonger and a knitwear store. Ten years ago, the village school from the 50s was almost closed down; it was saved by an influx of Polish and Romanian agricultural workers and their families. This year, the kindergarten is filled almost to capacity.

Some point toward the west, others toward the east

The wind shakes the big old house and the numerous trees forming the windbreak to its west. The house creaks dramatically. The 40-year-old wind chimes play along to the melody of an old hymn, 'Rise up, all things that God has made'. Slightly off-key. Five times each day, the old church, which has been here since the Valdemarians sometime in the 1200s, emits its automated chimes. The churchyard is three houses away. This is where much of her family resides. Some point toward the west, others toward the east. Knowing people at the church and so many in the churchyard – an overwhelming sense of belonging. She has spent a huge part of her childhood here: She thinks she knows every corner, every pothole in the road and the many windswept trees, all leaning toward the east. A both fascinating and claustrophobic sense of inhabiting a space between the past, present and future.

'Morning Glory'. The well-known melody awakens her from her slumber. She thought she could hear her almost 100-year-old maternal grandmother's crisp voice – but for the last 18 years, her grandmother has lain next to her grandfather in the churchyard soil. He was a head teacher, a parish clerk, who taught her to eat lard sandwiches with salt. He had a green office that smelled of books; not of althea bonbons (barley sugar), which she associates with the smell of her grandmother. The church bells break through the soundscape, whose main ingredient is otherwise the wind. Despite the howling of the wind, the place feels utterly tranquil. Waking up and hearing a car approaching. A branch tapping at the window. The sound of the place grows into her body. Living in and with soundscapes becomes part of her world-creation. She sits in the garden and listens; a tractor and some children on bikes passing by the driveway just before 8 am. The children returning home again at 2 pm. A truck spreading liquid manure passes on the road. The liquid stinks!

Smelling the environment and listening to sounds are different ways to sense. To sense is, in other words, to make sense. The surroundings attune her and she listens to the place's little stories. In one way, these stories are impersonal; they belong to collective situations, but they are experienced as personal.

The young soldiers' pale bottoms

The Germans occupied the school in 1943. They stayed in the classrooms and head teacher Wentzel, his wife and four children continued to live in the middle of the building. She has been told that her grandfather (teacher Wentzel) was smuggling letters addressed to members of the resistance movement in his daughter Marie's bag as she unknowingly wandered past the Germans in the schoolyard. In the spring of 1945, young soldiers – aged 17-18 – sat on their home-made latrines. Teacher Wentzel's two children, Marie and Karen (aged six and eight), stood giggling behind the trees, watching the young soldiers and their pale bottoms. Many years later, they remember how the sweet Hungarian soldier cried in Mrs Wentzel's lap when he had to go home. He had lost the war, but more than that, he had lost the gold watch his paternal grandmother had given him. Mrs Wentzel – the author's grandmother – found it and sent it to the address he had left behind. Maybe it reached its destination.

The bell tolls – the German soldiers marched south, and later German tourists would return in their yellow raincoats all along Jutland's West Coast. Past 'Ondaftenvej' (Evil Night Street), which must be one of the more bizarre street names in the area. At the car park by Husby Dune, only German cars can be seen on a windy September afternoon. Following the war, the Nazis left behind approximately 2000 bunkers, which were part of the Atlantic Wall – an extensive coastal defence line stretching from the North Cape to the Pyrenees in the south. For 70 years, the bunkers have lain on the beach, among the dunes, more or less covered by sand. Daubed with graffiti and colourful tags, there they lie, with their alluring entrances and small embrasures – a smell of urine, tar and salt. Now, most of them have been blown up and removed, or have been driven away in pieces. Is this History, stories or memories? The war is history: the Germans, the resistance, the bunkers. Memories are the girls' stories about the pale-skinned behinds.

Sand is drifting

The sea is still – calm. She observes Marie and Karen as they are unsteadily washed by the first waves – they make it past the surf. Swim in a state of bliss. They are now old women, aged 80 and 83. She supports them as they emerge from the sea. Later, they drink chilled white wine on the beach. They laugh. A handsome young man passes along the water's edge. They start to talk about love. The men in their lives pass by.

Kids on the beach: "Bury me!" they shout. One by one, they are buried in sand – only their heads remain visible. The sand is cold, and the kids do not stay submerged for long. Sand is everywhere. In every crack and crevice of the body. Sand between toes, in the car, in the hair. Sand from the landscape wanders into our beds. Crunches. The bell tolls. Time passes and time strikes. The wind blows; rows of tall, slender beech trees tremble graciously. Tempest Knud is raging.

Sea foam

The coordinates of the house mean that the North Sea is close by. The sea pulls her. The violent sea, with waves beating the shore. White Sea Foam all over, sticking to boots and settling like a spider's web. The rumble from the depths of the ocean. In 2012, the Danish rock band Nephew released a song "Hjertestarter" (defibrillator). They want the North Sea "to come and blow me into action". With a throbbing rhythm, the band shout at the sea. She loves to shout. Wild, loud – but a defibrillator heart starter is not needed here. For as long as she can remember, the sea has had a magical and irresistible calling for her. When she walks on the beach, over the dunes, or when she sleeps in the dunes on summer nights, she feels attached, or 'hefted' to the ground. According to Olwig (2007, p. 86) shepherds say the sheep heft or bond themselves to various places on the land, and also to the social unit called 'a heft'. She is not a sheep, but walking again and again on the beach, in the sand, in the wind, she feels rooted, tied (hefted) to and shaped by the land(scape).

Over the years, stones, shark eggs and decorative pieces of wood have been collected and taken back to the old school. The windowsill is dripping with objects that bring the beach and the landscape into the building, in the same way as the sand. On the windowsill, however, they lose some of their magic and part of their original life (like stones that become dull in comparison to the gleaming jewels gathered at the water's edge). Nevertheless, these objects become part of the family and family house as references to shared experiences – experiences and situations in a kind of family ecosystem (Rasmussen & Winther, forthcoming). Objects that appear in their natural habitat can seem vibrant and alive, and act as an echo or an evocative object from the past.

Becoming attuned

The flat, windblown landscape, the sea with the big waves and the long, deserted beach, sand, the atmosphere of a house. This landscape grows into her body as something embodied and felt. She thinks that many people's perceptions of and behaviour in specific places are shaped by some kind of implicit pre-understanding, like the grammar of your mother tongue. This grammar is learned and stored as a form of tacit knowledge – a kind of spatial grammar of the landscape that she carries in her. She allows herself to be lured and seduced. Allows the place to hone, mould and attune her.

The house breathes: Past, present, future, past, present, future … The atmosphere both is reminiscent of the past and embodies the present. The light is sharp though the window. It strikes the cupboard. Flickers and loses its sharpness, while placing her aboard a train of thought rolling into daydreams. To her, this house is an important place and, like other important places, it crawls into her gaze, emotions and perspectives. She is entangled in the material and immaterial aspects of inhabiting and getting comfortable with the surroundings. It is a strong topos, creating spirals of memories that move round and round, in-between, into cracks, in and out – in her consciousness, in her body, in how she gets lost and finds her way (Solnit 2006).

A house consists of specific spaces. The number may vary: the basement, the hallway, the kitchen, the labyrinth of corridors, bathrooms … these rooms can have a specific use, narrative status and grammar. All this will be specific to each user: we use the rooms differently, and this usage also varies across the many phases of life. Spaces speak and smell, but not all of us listen to the aural architecture (Blesser & Salter 2007) or use the olfactory experiences (Waskul & Vaninni 2008).

This house is huge and has so many sounds. It is old and has a special 'holiday-home odour', combined with the smell of salt and sand. It is an almost 100-year-old school, and built in accordance with the institutional architecture that was current at the time. As mentioned above, the concept 'schoolscape' can be used to denote the specific material and architectural signature that schools have. "Through our senses we measure the qualities of our surroundings – the tempo of life, the dominant patterns of color, texture, movement, and behavior – and these coalesce to make the world familiar or strange." (MacDougall 2006, p. 94) In 2020, there are no schoolchildren left. They moved to more modern premises 50 years ago. Nonetheless, she perceives the school's former life in the architecture, the large windows, the courtyard. Through the environment and the senses, she has been touched, smelled and heard into this specific sensory field.

The dwelling dwells

The place she inhabits can be like a cave: a somewhere in which she can daydream, where her ideas about the world are stored and developed, from where her world expands and to where she will always return. A prism that is able to shed light on the past and the future. This kind of place is more than a geographical location. From here, she takes care of something, confides in something. Perhaps the place also takes care of her. It is a structure loaded with meaning.

The dwelling dwells in her in the same way that she dwells in it. It comes imbued with the strength and the power of memory. Gaston Bachelard writes in *The Poetics of Space*: "…the house is one of the greatest powers of integration for the thoughts, memories and dreams of mankind. The binding principle in this integration is the daydream. Past, present and future give the house different dynamisms, which sometimes interfere, sometimes stimulate one another. In the life of man, the house thrusts aside contingencies, its councils of continuity are unceasing. Without it, man would be a dispersed being." (1994, pp. 6-7)

To dwell is to be closely interwoven with an experience of a certain place. The place becomes embedded in her capacity to dwell, be, see and remember. Such a place can be a place for 'homing oneself', understood as an ability to be in the world (Winther 2006, 2009). She learns 'to home' (as a verb, an action): to sense and make sense in her way through the world in finding herself.

If the table could speak

Her grandparents moved to another house across the street in 1969. A few years later, their children took over the school as a shared holiday home. Seventeen people sat around the long dining table every second weekend: Friday, pasta Bolognese; Saturday, fresh fish; Sunday, leftovers; and then back to everyday life. Late evenings, she could hear the adults playing cards while she and her sisters lay in their shared bunk bed. She could also hear the sounds of the martens that ran inside the cavity of the walls. As an adult, she has sometimes rested her ear against the wide, varnished dining table, trying to hear stories that the table has seen, heard, and remembered: serious conversations, gossip and mundane practices. The table has small grooves in which all manner of dirt has settled – cracks where small elements can be found, gathered together with memories of various people and things.

She walks though the old kitchen. Inside a cupboard, reminders and diaries from the 70s are taped up (a table of the people that have participated in the household). The tape erodes. The notes have hung there for decades without relevance, and point back to neat systems to ensure that the holiday home's finances were balanced, reasonable and fair. Today, these notes are an echo, a number of evocative objects.

Dried-out mummified frogs

The smell in the basement, where she finds dried-out mummified frogs every year, transports her back to her childhood. Bare feet on the steep stairs; the heavy trap door, which made it impossible to sneak down into the darkness for a soft drink. The sense of being caught in the sticky cobwebs, the crispy feeling of frogs crunching under her feet when she stepped on them, the smell of damp cement and old insulation materials, the taste of flat fizzy drinks long past their sell-by date. The thick, stuffy insulation is now porous, hanging by threads. This year's cobwebs will stick in her hair, unless she is supple enough to twist 180 degrees to turn on the water heater. Many types of sensory impressions and memories come together, across 45 years. According to Jennifer Mason: "Sensory memory is not about remembering a single sense experience, but about the memory of an atmosphere of multiple sensations." (2018, p. 44) Mason works in the slipstream of the French author Marcel Proust, where it is the taste of a Madeleine dipped in lime-blossom tea that recreates the closeness to a childhood room and sends the narrator, Marcel, on the path of lost time. In her holiday home, it is a damp basement that re-enacts such scenes and perceptions from distant, well-remembered and surprisingly vivid past times.

Losing her footing – selling the house

Time flies. The clock strikes. The chime is off-key. Nonetheless, the place is attuned, she is attuned. She loads up the car. She packs her bags, shuts down the house, and places her bags in the boot. They contain clothes, books and her computer. She always brings too much. Also, the emotional baggage weighs heavily (Löfgren 2016). How does she carry the emotional baggage with her, once she leaves? Where does she keep the sensory memory, which this exact place fills her with? In bags, in her photos, in her mind or body? Jennifer Mason keeps her father's ashes in an urn in her office. When Mason lets the ashes run through her fingers, the memories are awoken (2018, p. 13).

The estate agent is ready to put up the sign. The house has lost the function as a family anchor. It is too far away, too big to renovate. What happens to this memory when she can no longer hear the church bells? She has no ashes to let her fingers run through. Having to give up this place is like losing her footing, her direction, or losing herself. The bell tolls. She is driving away. So, for whom does the bell toll, indeed?

Exit:

In the text, memory occurs between the specific house, located in a specific region, with a family history attached to it, and me as a writer called she/her. I have tried to write about being, seeing and remembering a place. About belonging, echoes and memories as a way of finding ourselves – or losing ourselves. This holiday home functions as a crack; an in-between place between holiday and home; childhood and adulthood; past, present and future. It is blurred, repetitive and strange, like the collage based on private photos from the house taken in 2019*.

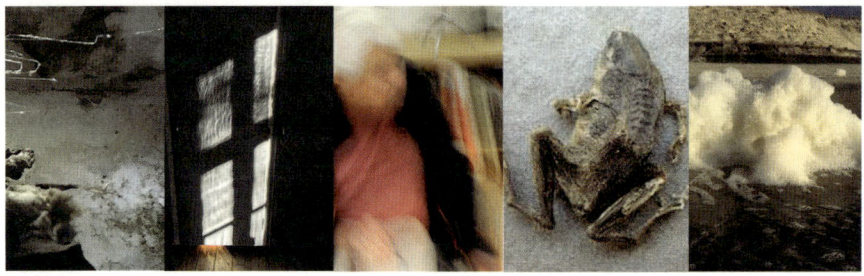

*In the summer of 2020, after finishing this chapter, I had second thoughts and bought the house. It was too heavy to carry in my bags and in my body alone.

References

Bachelard, G. (1994, [1957]). *The Poetics of Space*. Boston, Massachusetts: Beacon Press.

Blesser, B & Salter, L.R. (2007). *Spaces Speaks, Are You Listening?* Cambridge, Massachusetts: The MIT Press.

Ellis, C. (2003). *The Ethnographic I: A Methodological Novel about Autoethnography*. AltaMira Press.

Feld, S. & Basso, K.H. (1996). *Senses of Place*. Santa Fe: School of American Research Press.

Frykman, J. & Frykman, M.P. (2016). Affect and material culture. In *Sensitive Objects* (pp. 9-28). Lund: Nordic Academic Press.

Frykman, J. (2016). Done by inheritance – a phenomenological approach to affect and material culture. In Frykman, J. & Frykman, M.P. (Eds.) *Sensitive Objects* (pp. 153-76). Lund: Nordic Academic Press.

Ingold, T. & Vergunst, J. L. (2008). Introduction. In *Ways of Walking: Ethnography and Practice on Foot – Anthropological Studies of Creativity and Perception* (pp. 1-20). Aldershot: Ashgate.

Löfgren, O. (2016). Emotional baggage. In Frykman, J. & Frykman, M.P. (Eds.) *Sensitive Objects* (pp. 125-51). Lund: Nordic Academic Press.

MacDougall, D. (2006). *The Corporeal Image: Film, Ethnography, and the Sense*s. Princeton University Press.

MacDougall, D. (2007). *Schoolscapes*. London: Royal Anthropological Institute. Film.

Mason, J. (2018). *Affinities: Potent Connections in Personal Life*. Polity Press.

Olwig, K. R. (2008). Performing on the landscape versus doing landscape: perambulatory practice, sight and the sense of belonging. In Ingold, T. & Vergust, J.L. (Eds.) *Ways of Walking: Ethnography and Practice on Foot* (pp. 81-91). Aldershot: Ashgate.

Palludan, C. & Winther, I.W. (2016). 'Having my own room would be really cool': children's rooms as the social and material organizing of siblings. *Journal of Material Culture* 22 (1), 34-50.

Proust, M. (1963, [1920]). À la recherche du temps perdu published in seven volumes, previously translated as Remembrance of Things Past (1913-1927). *På sporet af den tabte tid*. Copenhagen: Martins Forlag.

Rasmussen, J. D. & Winther, I. W. (in process). Sensory Loss and the Notion of Family Ecologies.

Schafer, R. M. (1977). *The Soundscape: Our Sonic Environment and the Tuning of the World*. Alfred Knopf.

Solnit, R. (2005). *A Field Guide to Getting Lost*. Penguin Books.

Stewart, K. (2007). *Ordinary Affects*. Duke University Press.

Turkle, S. (2007). *Evocative Objects – Things We Think With*. Cambridge: The MIT Press.

Waskul, D. & Vaninni, P. (2008). Smell, odor, and somatic work: sense-making and sensory management. *Social Psychology Quarterly* 71 (1), 53-71.

Winther, I.W. (1996). En bliven hjem: 'Die Zweite Heimat' i skæret af Gilles Deleuzes filmteori. In Kyndrup, M. & Lehmann, N. (Eds.) *Formelle rum: Æstetikstudier lll*. (pp.119-46). Aarhus: Aarhus Universitetsforlag.

Winther, I. W. (2006). *Hjemlighed: kulturfænomenologiske studier*. Copenhagen: Danmarks Pædagogiske Universitetsforlag.

Winther, I. W. (2009). Homing oneself: home as a practice. *Haecceity Papers* 4 (2), 49-83.

Winther, I.W. (2013). Children's everyday lives (re)constructed as variable sets of 'field bodies' – Revisiting the 'exotic' remote island – a case study. *Nordic Studies in Education*, 2, 112-23.

Winther, I.W. (2018). Det upåagtedes etnografi – feltvandring og sanselige metoder som etnografiske tilgange i undersøgelsen af 'ik' noget. In Jensen, H.L. & Jacobsen, M.H. (Eds.) *Etnografier* (pp. 297-323). Copenhagen: Hans Reitzels Forlag.

AFTERWORD:

The micro-physics of mornings

Orvar Löfgren

What is actually going on when nothing seems to happen? And how do we get to know? Reading the stimulating contributions to this book is like a journey through unnoticed and seemingly insignificant everyday phenomena. We may choose different labels for them – in-betweens, cracks, pockets, non-events – and such moments can seem very personal, but they are, as the authors show, at the same time intensely cultural and social and this makes them a rewarding field of study for the social and cultural sciences. By shifting attention to situations and settings that often slip through the fingers in attempts to capture everyday life, new terrains and analytical connections open up. As the texts show, it is precisely in these seemingly insignificant situations that there is a chance to grasp important elements in the usually unnoticed undercurrents of everyday life. We are shown how in-betweens are shaped, given form, content and colour through the entanglements of movements, routines, feelings and moods, as well as through bodies and artefacts, but we are also given a toolbox for getting at these often invisible phenomena. Each chapter illustrates different analytical approaches to the topic, and different styles of bringing them to life in writing.

Reading the texts, I begin to reflect on my own experiences of in-betweens, and a powerful memory surfaces. It is an early September morning and I am driving through a rural landscape on my way to a conference, hours away. The stillness is total, there is no traffic; just the intense sun, me, the morning programme on the car radio and a landscape waking up to a new day. Now and then along the empty road I pass school children waiting for the bus, some on their own, others in groups. There is a such a strong feeling of in-betweenness here, not only the *terrains vagues* of bus stops, silent woodlands and empty fields in the middle of nowhere, but also the feeling of *temps vague*. Is anything really happening here? Some of the kids are busy with their phones; others just stare out into space, or talk to each other. This is the special mood of waiting, a vague feeling of being on standby. Like those who are waiting, I am also in transit, *here* – in an in-between – but mentally elsewhere.

Although the in-between is used as an open and exploratory concept in this book, it has special potentials as it often describes a movement or a situation of transit – a kind of liminality. It can be waiting for something to start, going through the routines of getting ready for something else, being transported from one point or project to another. This creates an interesting vagueness or openness. As the contributors point out, many in-betweens in daily life are hard to capture and verbalize, which calls for experimental ethnographies, the trying out of different approaches. I would like to explore these possibilities a little further, continuing to use morning experiences as my theme.

But first of all, some more general reflections. A cultural analysis of everyday life needs to focus on break points, transitions and cracks – words that catch different aspects of in-betweenness. I find the discussion of "pocket ethnography" in the introductory chapter very rewarding, because it encompasses both spatial and temporal compartments as in-betweens, but also because it turns the attention to mental and material entanglements (a theme explored in different ways by Ingold (2011) and Hodder (2012)).

I would also like to draw attention to some other approaches to processes of intertwining – for example, what the cultural geographer Doreen Massey (2005) has termed *throwntogetherness:* the ways in which materialities, bodies, sensibilities, feelings and activities co-exist. Her concept explores how diverse elements come to cohabit in a setting or a situation, often as unexpected neighbours, which calls for ongoing processes of confrontation, negotiation and accommodation.

Analysing a special situation or setting, we need to ask what is thrown together and what we might overlook. Like many of the chapters in this book, I would like to start with materiality. The anthropologist Danny Miller reminds us that objects are important, not because they are evident and mentally present but quite the opposite: it is often precisely because we do not *see* them. The less we are aware of them, the more they influence our actions and expectations. Objects work by being invisible and unmarked and simply taken for granted (Miller 2009, p 50).

In a given setting, things co-habit in ways that give them transformative powers.

In her book *Vibrant Matter,* Jane Bennett (2010) analyses the agency and affective power of things, from a small collection of rubbish to a nationwide electricity grid, using Deleuze and Gattari's term *assemblage*. Maurizia Boscagli (2014) also tackles similar issues of affect and materiality. Approaches like these explore affects as potentially energising or intensifying in the everyday life of things. Things are joined into a "confederate agency", or a "vibrant assemblage", as Bennett puts it. She points out that an assemblage owes its capacity for agency to the "shi" effect, a Chinese term that describes something that is hard to verbalize:

> *… the kind of potential that originates not in human initiative but instead results from the very disposition of things.* Shi *is the style, energy, propensity, trajectory or élan inherent to a specific arrangement of things.* (Bennett 2010, p. 35)

Stuff is a special category of *shi*, often vague, liminal and overwhelming. It is things on the move (Boscagli 2014, pp. 5ff). At home, pockets of stuff are found everywhere – for example, on the top shelves in the kitchen where domestic driftwood gathers, projects and stuff that have been abandoned or forgotten. Jean Claude Kaufmann (2012) has analysed another kind of powerful assemblage: all the things crowded together in the dark depths of the handbag; while Christena Nippert-Eng (2010) has explored the secrets of the wallet. There are silent corners, domestic side roads and backwaters that create pockets, but also all kinds of temporal pockets, situations of liminality, stasis or inertia. And not forgetting the ways in which breaks and pauses reorganize and recharge life at work or at home (see Ehn & Löfgren 2012).

If the role of artefacts was, for a long time, overlooked in the ethnographies of everyday life, the same goes for another, often unnoticed dimension that is also explored in this book: that of affect, moods and atmosphere and the ways in which they connect and interact with material objects. "The affective turn" (Gregg and Seigworth 2010) has been with us now for some time, but it is striking that research in this area has often lacked an ethnographic approach, which can lead us to understand how affect actually works in the mundane. Kathleen Stewart (2017, p. 194) has pointed out that the interest in affect has vitalised the study of materiality, generating an interest in sense and sensation.

George Downing discusses the importance of looking at what he calls "micro-practices" in order to understand the relations between affect, emotion and movement (2000, p. vii). Downing is thinking about the capacity to sense a feeling, letting it evolve or change, using it as a lens to explore a situation and maybe later putting it into words. He points to the importance of affects to create movement, that they have a potential for change. A sudden feeling may stop an activity, signal a change, create a new focus – it puts us in a state of "action readiness". Affect may thus be momentary or fleeting, and may develop into a more long-lived emotion as affects are verbalized and culturally interpreted (see the discussion in Frykman & Frykman 2016, pp. 16ff; Löfgren 2015 and Wetherell 2012, pp. 120ff).

Everyday activities are saturated by affects, which usually start as something unconscious and pre-discursive. It might be a tingling sensation, a sudden itch or a vague sense of foreboding. Legs get restless, muscles contract, and a sense of unease makes the body want to shift positions. All of a sudden there is a need to move somewhere else, either mentally or physically. Affects take shape, create rhythms, timings, vibrancy or energy. Strong affects contain a push to do something, to move away or move closer, as Margaret Wetherell (2012, p. 29) has put it.

Kathleen Stewart has pointed out that everyday life is full of what she calls "mood work", a concept focusing on the ways in which senses and the world coexist. "Mood work marshals bodies, objects, technologies, sensations and flights of fancy into forms of partial coherence … They press, promise, enfold, and power worlds being thrown together." (Carlson & Stewart 2014, p. 114). In mood work, there is a constant traffic of movements and sensations between bodies, minds and the material environment. It is about modes of being in the world; it is about feelings, moods and rhythms, as well as performativity and sensibilities. In this sense there is a strong focus on the affective dimensions of everyday life, the in-betweenness not only between human actors but also between humans and objects. Mood work is a concept that is a useful analytical partner of *throwntogetherness*.

If materialities and affects are elements that need to be brought into the foreground, this also goes for routinisation, a process that helps to produce the invisibility and insignificance of in-betweens and non-events. Routines turn them into something taken for granted, slowly sinking into the body and becoming "mere reflexes". Routinisation helps to make activities and tasks not merely invisible but frequently defined as unimportant. Routines are about economising, tacit agreements, indirect negotiations, cutting corners. This is about the half-said, the shrug, the nod. Social and emotional messages go back and forth, often without being put into words. I would like to take such microphysics of everyday life into the ethnography of mornings.

Morning in-betweens

In interviewing people for a project on routines (Ehn & Löfgren 2010), we found that people often started by talking about their morning habits, and this was not only because it felt like a natural narrative start. Morning routines are about staggering from sleep to waking and getting body and mind ready for the outside world. Mornings are vulnerable times and routines become an important survival strategy; a number of small tasks have to be coordinated, sequenced or multitasked. Getting ready to move and prepare yourself for another day calls for the gathering of energy and some focus. Mornings are also organised as transitions, which create different kinds of in-betweenness.

Several researchers have pointed to the strong charge in the ingrained habits of everyday mornings. The French sociologist Jean-Claude Kaufmann (1997, p. 19) talks about the "morning dance" of going through all the necessary preparations for taking off out into the world. Body and mind are constantly working and it is often the hands that lead the way: reaching for the bar of soap in the shower, pouring coffee while turning the pages of the morning paper, rummaging through drawers for a missing sock.

What is so loaded about morning routines, asks the sociologist Christina Nippert-Eng in her interview study of how Americans organise their lives between home and work. In getting ready for a new working day, routines may work as a warming up, she says. They make the shifts between the daily moves between home and work easier. The mindless activities prepare us for the mindful ones (Nippert-Eng 1995, pp. 113ff.). For some, this passage is always demanding and calls for some small tricks of mental reframing.

Mornings are also about the coordination of micro-movements under the pressure of time. Sometimes mornings are described as effortless, taking an almost sleepwalking body through the many tasks thanks to a perfectly functioning autopilot. However, running out of time also calls for sudden improvisation, and in skipping some routines or making shortcuts a strongly interwoven patchwork of routines is destabilised. Thus, some mornings turn chaotic or become full of tensions. Synchronisation between household members fails, priorities clash; there are angry knocks on the bathroom door, heated arguments about who should take the dog out, and the kitchen table is left a mess for the person who comes last to breakfast. There are frantic searches for the cell phone charger or that lost memo from work. This is where the system breaks down. Morning routines are not just pre-choreographed but danced, with constant improvisations.

If you want to study how micro-moves are embodied in routines, rituals and in-betweens, mornings are therefore not a bad place to start. In getting ready for a new day, movements, affect, sensations and stuff all interact in the making and unmaking of practices. Morning time means quick movements from station to station, with changing micro-climates. Certain spaces and activities carry a strong element of in-betweenness. The bathroom is a good example of this. For many, the minutes in the shower offer a chance of some solitary daydreaming, an activity helped by the flow of the warm water. The sensual and meditative mood of shaving or putting on make-up in front of the mirror offers a chance to contemplate what kind of day lies ahead. "Those ten minutes in front of the mirror are the most important moment of the day," says one woman. While her hands rummage through her make-up bag and a lipstick colour is chosen, she carries on an inner dialogue between herself and the changing image in the mirror. Deft micro-movements are combined with fast mind-travel.

Mornings are full of such processes. It can be some diffuse anxiety about the day ahead, a nervous energy seeking an outlet. It takes a quick movement to get out of bed (on the right side), or an extra minute in the shower to handle that. It might be a sudden feeling of enthusiasm, which starts to overflow and create new mobilities of ideas, objects and people (see Hui 2014, p. 179). Affects flow between the rooms, turn into building materials of moods and lead to quick changes in atmosphere – around the kitchen table, for example. Affect is often discussed in terms of an assessment of intensities, but Lauren Berlant reminds us not to overlook minor moods that are sensed rather than known:

> *… most social life happens in such modes of lowercase dramas, as we follow the pulsating habituated patterning that makes possible getting through the day (the relationships, the job, the life) while the brain chatters on, assessing things in focused and unfocused ways.* (Berlant 2008, p. 6)

In all mood work, there is a constant traffic of movements and sensations between bodies, minds and the material environment. Sounds, smells, tastes and light flow through the morning. The sensory tools of the body are sent out on quick journeys and return with impacts: the protective warmth of the bed against the cool hardness of the floor, the invigorating smell of coffee travelling through the house, the inviting softness of the sofa. There are the angry red blips of gadgets demanding to be charged in the kitchen dusk, or the ways in which the first rays of the morning sun travel through the rooms, changing the atmosphere.

The different senses combine to handle tasks and moves. Eyes listen carefully as hands see in the dark, and there is a bitter feeling in the mouth when waking up after a bad dream. In studying the work of the senses, the tactile dimensions are often underrepresented, as Jennifer Mason (2018) and Constance Classen (2012) have pointed out. In morning activities, the kinaesthetic and haptic dimensions are important, coordinating impressions and body moves, registering textures, vibrations, temperature, pressure or resistance; touching and being touched as one navigates through the morning world.

Some morning activities are so important that they are cemented into important habits, which cannot just be skipped or overlooked. In this process they may also become ritualised and thereby acquire a moral or emotional charge. In a way, many of these quick steps are like small *rites de passage*, signalling transformations or situations of inclusion or exclusion, togetherness or privacy.

The power of the unnoticed

Mornings can be seen as an encompassing in-between, a moving from sleep to a new working day, but they also contain many examples of small in-betweens, pockets and passages. There are moments of stress as well as of stillness, with changing rhythms and moods. They are framed by constricted spaces, time limits and everyday repetitions. Ordinary mornings contain a heavily charged set of micro-movements, and the time pressure calls for keen coordination, synchronization and multi-tasking. Patchworks of practices are stitched together. Affect and emotions charge these seemingly trivial activities.

Routines sink into the body and many of them cannot be questioned, they have simply become "just me". This gives them power, while questions about priorities, hierarchy and control lurk in the background and may turn into angry discussions and frustrations. The hidden moral economy of the household surfaces in such emotionally laden situations (Löfgren 2016). What are those towels doing on the bathroom floor? Why isn't there any coffee left?

When studying routines, it is easy to get stuck in the reassuring idea of a constantly repeated pattern. If we look at the transformations of making and unmaking, another more dynamic picture emerges. It is important to look closer for traces of the subversive potential of routines, as this aspect is probably not the first thing that comes to mind in connection with inconspicuous repetitive behaviour. But when one examines the ordinary ways of everyday life, hour by hour, day after day, one might find that these seemingly repetitive acts may, in fact, produce small and successive changes, hardly perceptible but possibly important in the long run. What one sees as "the same procedure as usual" does not have to be that repetitive at all. It may hide some surprising and subversive transformations.

In Jonathan Safran Foer's 2016 novel *Here I Am*, we follow the couple Julia and Jacob. When Julia and Jacob got married, they created new routines: "Everything seemed to move toward ritual." (Foer 2016, p. 12) Morning routines were an important part of this construction work, a web of mundane tasks and rituals that bind the couple together. Step by step they turn their new life together into a domestic world of invisible habits. Such routines may take the shape of small gestures and tasks that show caring. As Julia and Jacob get ready to go out into the world, their preparations are full of such micro-rituals of reassurance and love. Julia takes a shower first, while Jacob puts the breakfast on the table. She always pours the first cup of coffee for him; he gets the morning paper and passes her the section he knows she wants to start with. She gives him a kiss as he leaves the house.

But gradually, the morning routines start to change. Foer depicts how Julia and Jacob's marriage begins to erode by focusing on all the seemingly unimportant changes: "Time passed, the world exerted itself, and Jacob and Julia began to forget to do things on purpose." The cherished routines and rituals were all still there, but slowly "the inside of life became far smaller than the outside, creating a cavity, an emptiness." (Foer 2016, p. 15) Julia forgets to pour his coffee, and Jacob starts to pick his own favourite part of the newspaper first. And that morning kiss? Maybe it can wait until tomorrow. Small, unconscious transformations that signal a major change. It is in the dismantling of the small routines that the breakdown of their marriage is taking place. The habits of the partner, which once seemed so charming, begin to get irritating. The cherished ritual movements slowly turn into mere mechanical reflexes. The eroding routines signal a new but still invisible journey: that of breaking up a home. It is a changing flow of energy that the novelist depicts. Trivial arguments about the morning routines – the loading of the dishwasher or turning the thermostat up – may really be about something much larger. Inconspicuous acts can turn into provocations. Routines thus become sites of struggle and domination, but also of resistance. People drag their feet, defend old routines, forget things or ignore cues. Again, it is the subtlety in the power play in such activities that is important. The strong weapon of indirectness is at work here – a special kind of micro-politics, where what is seen as a "non-event" may turn out to be hiding something very eventful. There is another power dimension here. People are going through the same motions, but something is happening; what is seen as stasis or mere repetition may hide changes with a subversive potential.

Thomas O'Dell (2006) has borrowed the phrase *backdraft* from firefighters: a fire is hidden in a smouldering, invisible ember in a closed room; everything seems as usual until someone opens the door and allows in the oxygen that then causes the fire to explode. Looking for cultural backdrafts, we can find silent situations in which a mere side remark, an afterthought or an action can act as a catalyst, making a routine flare up into something else.

In the contributions to this book, there are many surprising insights into the undercurrents of the everyday. Each chapter offers different ethnographic approaches and experiments. A school setting, where the seemingly insignificant breaks shape affinities and senses of belonging; a day care playground, where the basic element of sand offers ways of creating connections and sensing the world. Public situations, like a wheelchair skating event, illustrate the importance of rhythms – of being in and out of sync, for example. Or an alchemical ethnography of elderly people handling the city and connecting to the urban scene in very different ways. The book includes two very personal ethnographies, the intense bodily connections between mother and child during maternity leave, and an archaeology of memories layered in a house, creating a special "grammar of place". These explorations show the advantages of moving closer to a situation, setting or phenomenon, and of just keeping on looking. Surprising insights can be made by poking into corners, listening intently to silences, sensing passing moods, rummaging through pockets of all kinds, and exploring the stillness of backyards or choosing a side door instead of a main entrance.

References

Bennett, J. (2011). *Vibrant Matter. A Political Ecology of Things*. Durham: Duke University Press.

Berlant, L. (2008). Thinking about feeling historical. *Emotion, Space and Society*, 1 (1), 4-9.

Boscagli, M. (2014). *Stuff Theory. Everyday Objects and Radical Materialism*. London: Bloomsbury.

Carlson, J. D. & Stewart, K. C. (2014). The legibilities of mood work. *New Formations*, 114-33.

Classen, C. (2012). *The Deepest Sense. A History of Touch.* Urbana: University of Illinois Press.

Downing, G. (2000). Emotion theory reconsidered. In Wrathall, M. & Malpas, J. (Eds.), *Heidegger, Coping and Cognitive Science* (pp. 245-70). Cambridge: MIT Press.

Edensor, T. (2014). Rhythm and arrhythmia. In Adey, P. et al. (Eds.), *The Routledge Handbook of Mobilities* (pp. 163-71). London: Routledge.

Ehn, B. & Löfgren, O. (2010). *The Secret World of Doing Nothing.* Berkeley: University of California Press.

Ehn, B. & Löfgren, O. (2012). Pausens mikrodramatik. En essä om önskade och oönskade avbrott. *Sosiologi idag* 42 (1), 15-36.

Frykman, J. & Frykman, M.P. (2016): Affect and Material Culture. Perspectives and Strategies. In *Sensitive Objects. Affect and Material Culture* (pp. 9-30). Lund: Nordic Academic Press.

Gregg, M. & Seigworth, G.J. (2010) *The Affect Theory Reader* (pp. 29-51). Durham: Duke University Press.

Hodder, I. (2012). *Entangled. An Archaeology of the Relationships between Humans and Things.* Oxford: Wiley Blackwell.

Hui, A. (2014): Enthusiasm. In Adey, P. et al. (Eds.), *The Routledge Handbook of Mobilities* (pp. 172-82). London: Routledge.

Ingold, T. (2011). *Being Alive: Essays on Movement, Knowledge and Description.* London: Routledge.

Kaufmann, J.-C. (1997): *Le cœur à l'ouvrage. Théorie de l'action ménagère.* Paris: Nathan.

Kaufmann, J.-C. (2012). *Privatsache Handtasche.* Munich: UVK.

Löfgren, O. (2015). Catching a Mood. In Ehn, B., Löfgren, O. & Wilk, R. (Eds.) *Exploring Everyday Life* (pp. 81-98). Lanham: Rowman and Littlefield.

Löfgren, O. (2019). Mine or ours? The home as a moral economy. In Braun, K., Dieterich, C.-M., Moser, J. & Schönholz, C. (Eds.), *Wirtschaften. Kulturwissenschaftliche Perspektiven* (pp. 15-35). Marburg: Philipps-Universität. https://archiv.ub.uni-marburg.de/es/2019/0032/pdf/makufee-s-01.pdf

Mason, J. (2018). *Affinities – Potent Connections in Personal Life.* Cambridge: Polity Press.

Massey, D. (2005). *For Space.* London: Sage.

Miller, D. (2010). *Stuff.* Cambridge: Polity Press.

Nippert-Eng, C. (1995). *Home and Work.* Chicago: University of Chicago Press.
Nippert-Eng, C. (2010). *Islands of Privacy.* Chicago: University of Chicago Press.
O'Dell, T. (2006). Cultural Back-Draft. In Löfgren, O. & Wilk, R. (Eds.), *Off the Edge. Experiments in Cultural Analysis (pp. 44-49).* Copenhagen: Museum Tusculanum Press. (Also as special issue of *Ethnologia Europaea* 35, No. 1-2.)
Stewart, K. (2017). In the World That Affect Proposed. *Cultural Anthropology* 32 (2), 192-8.
Wetherell, M. (2015). *Affect and Emotion. A New Social Science Understanding.* London: Sage.

Author information

Karen Ida Dannesboe, PhD, associate professor at Danish School of Education, Aarhus University

Jon Dag Rasmussen, PhD, assistant professor at Department of the Built Environment, Aalborg University

Naja Dahlstrup Mogensen, MA in Educational Anthropology & PhD Student at Danish School of Education, Aarhus University

Nanna Jordt Jørgensen, PhD, associate professor at University College Copenhagen

Anne-Lene Sand, PhD, postdoctoral researcher at Design School Kolding

Ida Wentzel Winther, PhD, associate professor at Danish School of Education, Aarhus University

Orvar Löfgren, PhD, Professor Emeritus at University of Lund